Helping Children to Write

Helping Children to Write

by Ann Browne

P·C·P

Paul Chapman
Publishing Ltd

Reprinted 2002

Paul Chapman Publishing Ltd
144 Liverpool Road
London
N1 1LA

British Library Cataloguing in Publication Data
Browne, Ann
  Helping Children to Write.
  I. Title II. Series
  372.6
ISBN 1 85396 224 4

Typeset by Hewer Text Composition Services, Edinburgh
Printed and bound in Great Britain by
Biddles Ltd., Guildford and King's Lynn

  E F G H   9

Contents

Acknowledgements

Many experiences and people contribute to an author's ability to write a book and I would like to thank the many people, children and schools that have shaped my thinking and provided me with the insights and experience that are expressed in this book. I would especially like to thank Ruth Grindrod, who provided a great deal of help with the whole book and who contributed greatly to Chapters 7 and 8, dealing with bilingualism, gender and writing. The children who provided most of the writing illustrated in this book were pupils at Berger Infant School, Hackney, Frettenham First School, Norfolk, and Kingsmead Primary School, Hackney.

In particular, this book is dedicated to the children of the schools in the London Borough of Hackney in which I worked. They taught me a great deal. More generally this book has been written for all children everywhere who deserve the best education that can be offered to them.

Introduction

The purpose of this book is to provide an introductory text about young children's writing for students, teachers, teachers on in-service courses, governors and parents. It outlines recent developments in writing and describes classroom practices that match current understanding of the process of learning to write. It has grown out of my experience of working with children aged between four and eight years of age in a variety of classroom settings. Wherever possible, links have been made in the text between the theory and the practice of writing and many of the points made in the text are illustrated with examples of children's writing arising from my work in the classroom.

The book began its life in response to requests from teachers who wanted to know more about how to implement developmental writing in schools. When the National Curriculum for English suggested a developmental approach to writing, many teachers were unfamiliar with working in this way. The National Curriculum is now four years old but there is still a need to explain what a developmental approach to writing means, what it involves and how it can be implemented in the classroom. There is still some confusion about how to teach writing developmentally, particularly amongst students, parents and governors as well as teachers. Currently developmental writing and the practices outlined in this book have been given credibility by the National Curriculum and I have indicated this wherever possible in the text.

The book begins with a chapter that examines the developments that have led to a greater understanding of what writing is for and what writers do when they write. This provides the context within which a developmental approach to writing is set. Chapter 2 looks at the development of children's writing that occurs over time when teachers take account, when they are teaching writing, of what children know and can do. Chapter 3 presents a variety of activities and practices that teachers can use as they work developmentally with young writers. Chapters 4 and 5 examine the teaching of spelling and handwriting. The issue of assessment is currently very topical and Chapter 6 examines what to assess and how to assess in the light of the requirements of the National Curriculum and of good practice. Chapter 7 looks at how a developmental approach to writing matches the needs of bilingual pupils as learners of English. Recently the issue of the different needs of girls and boys as writers has been receiving more attention and Chapter 8 presents some suggestions for teachers who are concerned to cater for the needs of all their pupils. We would all acknowledge that parents and carers can and do play a major part in children's education and Chapter 9 specifically examines the contribution that parents can make to the writing development of children. The final chapter presents a sample writing policy for schools to use or adapt as they wish. I hope that this will be useful to teachers who are writing or updating a policy statement for their school. Apart from Chapters 1 and 10, each chapter ends with a number of questions and answers related to the theme of that chapter. These have arisen from workshops with teachers, parents and students and attempt to deal with particular queries that have been voiced. Whilst many of the questions may have been dealt with in the chapter, the answers provide more detailed and specific guidance on aspects of developmental writing. Although the intention of this book is to present a detailed consideration of developmental writing it is not exhaustive and for further reading and information the reader is referred to the bibliography.

Throughout the book both the child and the teacher are referred to as *she* except when specific children or adults are mentioned or quoted. In these cases the children and people are denoted by their actual gender and the terms *he* and *she* are used as appropriate.

In this book I have tried to represent the best of current practice as it is known at present. It may change and develop; future research and practice may provide further insights into our understanding of what writing is and how it is learned. Good practice is never static: it responds to new thinking, new needs and particular situations. It develops as we try to understand learning and then develop teaching to accommodate new insights about learning. I hope that this book provides some ideas that enable practitioners to reflect on and extend their practice so that they can follow the advice of Temple *et al.* (1988): 'Let children know you treasure language, and they'll treasure it also. Help them understand, as early as possible, that language is theirs to manipulate and they'll respond. There's no magical ingredient that gets children to write.'

Ann Browne
March 1993

1

Writing is . . .

Introduction

This chapter examines some of the research and investigations into writing that have taken place over the last decade. It looks at how this has contributed to changes in the way that the teaching of writing is viewed.

The chapter is divided into three sections: 'The nature of writing', 'Young children learning about writing', and 'Implications for teaching'. 'The nature of writing' considers the significance of writing and its distinctive features as a form of communication. 'Young children learning about writing' examines the knowledge that many children have about writing when they begin school and offers a developmental model of young children's early writing ability. This section indicates how children's competence in producing writing expands with increasing acquaintance with models of writing and opportunities to practise writing. The final section, 'Implications for teaching', attempts to draw together an understanding of writing and an understanding of young children as literacy learners to provide a framework for the effective teaching of writing.

The final section is expanded and examined in subsequent chapters of this book. Before embarking on the details of planning a writing curriculum for young children it is important to have some understanding of the nature of what one is teaching and the learner's understanding of the task. If one understands writing and writing development then effective teaching may be possible.

The nature of writing

Children are immersed in literature, in its widest sense, and surrounded by print almost from the day they are born. Their presence in the world is acknowledged when their birth is officially recorded. For many children the event of their birth is marked further by a printed announcement in the newspaper and parents receiving cards and letters of congratulation. Children are born into a world that is filled with evidence of our literate society both in the home and in the wider environment. Writing is found on signs, notices, advertising hoardings, timetables, shops and the television screen as well as in books and newspapers. The list is endless. It is true to say that babies, children and adults are surrounded by print. No one can fail to notice that writing is a significant component of life in the twentieth century.

Why is writing important? What are the purposes of writing? When parents put an announcement of a child's birth in the newspaper they are telling friends, relatives and acquaintances that something significant has occurred. They are communicating facts about the new baby, her date of birth, her name and their pleasure in her arrival, efficiently and succinctly to a large group of people. Letters and cards of congratulation sent in response to the announcement are again acts of communication signalling pleasure and interest in what has occurred. Both the announcement and the responses are pieces of writing that have been undertaken with a particular purpose, audience and method of distribution in mind. One of the reasons that writing is important in our lives is because it is a communicative act that transmits information and links people together.

Writing can be used in many ways. It can be used to satisfy material needs, to persuade, to suggest and indicate appropriate behaviour and responses, to establish contact with others, to express one's individuality, to question, to explore, to clarify and organize thoughts, to reflect, to exercise the imagination, to communicate information, to evaluate, to entertain and to provide a record of events or ideas. As Willig (1990) states,

> Writing is a key element in the search for meaning because it allows us to reflect on and to order our encounters with the world and the impact they make upon us. Equally importantly, we write to share thoughts and feelings with others through communications ranging from hastily written notes to formal, carefully argued essays on complex issues.
>
> (Willig, 1990, p. 25)

The uses of writing identified above might also be seen as the uses of speaking. Speaking and writing can perform similar functions; writing can do everything that language in general can do, as Smith (1982) points out: 'Writing can be an extension and reflection of all our efforts to develop and express ourselves in the world around us, to make sense of the world and to impose order upon it.'

Goodman (1990) stresses the importance of the similarities between oral and written language for young children who are learning about writing. She suggests that by understanding this relationship children may come to realize some of the forms and functions of writing. That writing is related to oral language may seem clear to the adults but how do children learn this? Through experience with print, in the world and in stories, children do begin to understand the relationship between oral and written language and they may demonstrate this in their early attempts at writing. As children play with paper and writing implements they often produce their first attempts at writing. They may show these to an adult and request that these are read back to them, asking 'What does this say?' When they do this they are demonstrating that they are aware that language has a written symbol form and that the meaning that written symbols carry may be retrieved and communicated orally. Additional evidence of the development of understanding that oral and written language are related has been provided by Bussis, Chittenden and Klausner (1985) who have reported that before children can read unaided they know that stories are represented in books and that these can be recovered orally. When looking at books young children will often follow a text, repeating and constructing aloud a story that is familiar to them, before they can read each word that is written.

Perhaps, because teachers wish to simplify the process of learning to write, they often stress the similarities between speaking and writing to young children rather than explaining the differences as well. If children are led to believe that everything that can be written can be spoken they may see little point in learning to write. All teachers can recount stories of children who can tell magnificent tales but who, when it comes to writing their story down, produce two static, misspelt sentences. A six-year-old girl in an infant classroom was recently overheard saying, 'I want to work in Tesco when I'm older because you don't have to write.' The children cited in these examples do not seem to have established any reasons for writing that are relevant to their present lives nor have they gained any understanding of how writing can extend their communicative competence.

Writing is different to oral language; it is not just speech that is written down. There is a great deal of difference between the minutes of a meeting and what was actually said there or between a written telephone message and what the caller has said. In the words of Czerniewska (1992), writing and speaking 'have to be seen as functioning in different ways'. Writing is not dependent on the presence of the audience nor is it linked to context as spoken language often is. It can communicate with large numbers of people over an extended period of time. It can be retrieved by the author and the recipient long after the message was initiated and can allow communication to take place without the simultaneous presence of both parties. As writing is always recorded it can form a permanent record and enable the writer to remember ideas or items. The tangible form of writing encourages reflection on what one is trying to communicate and allows the author to work on the way that ideas are expressed. It can be planned, revised and organized to convey what is meant with precision. Writing is a craft that may involve the writer in focusing, planning, organizing, reflecting and revising what is being written in order to produce a product that is suited to its purpose and audience. Not all of these processes are necessary for all writing that is undertaken – for example a note to the milk deliverer requires a different approach to that taken when writing an application for a job – but one of the skills of writing is to be able to select those aspects of the process that are suited to the task. Knowledge about writing and how to write can give people some control over what is communicated. The writer can make choices about what is and what is not communicated and how to present the content of what is communicated.

Writing is a significant feature of life in the twentieth century. It surrounds and affects everyone. It can be a powerful means of communication, on occasion more powerful than speech, since it may give the user and the recipient time to reflect on what is being communicated. Time and opportunities for reflection offer the writer power over how a message is transmitted and what information that message contains.

Young children learning about writing

Before they start school, children learn many things that are pertinent to their learning to become writers. They learn to become adept users of language in its oral form and they learn about the presence and use of writing in the home and in the world.

Initially children use oral language to gain attention and to have their needs met. Later, language becomes a way not only of giving information but also of receiving it. Children seem to be driven by the need to talk and question and to enter into dialogues with others. They want to give and receive information and language is one way that makes this possible. As they speak and listen they become familiar with language as a system. They use and interpret the semantic, syntactic and phonic elements of language. They know that language makes sense, that in order for it to make sense it is organized in a particular way, and that it draws on a set of sound symbols. They can use language in different ways to suit different audiences. For example, they are unlikely to talk to a grandparent in the same way as they talk to a friend. They respond differently, and generally appropriately, to the different ways in which language is addressed to them. They use language to express needs and emotions, to persuade, to question, to initiate and to conclude a dialogue. By the time most children start school they are adept and competent users of language in its oral form. This provides a starting point for learning about other forms of language.

Young children also learn 'large amounts of information relevant to growing up in our culture' (Tizard and Hughes, 1984). Through communication, experience and observation they learn about their environment, the people and objects within it and the routines that form part of daily living. They learn about what is significant, valued and used by the adults around them. Children seem to want to be like those around them and to this end they imitate the behaviour of family members. Since writing is a prevalent and significant feature of life in the twentieth century it is likely that all children will see its presence and use in the home and the environment. As children recognize that writing is a form of communication, as they see others writing and as they see examples of writing around them, they seem to want to write and to begin to experiment with writing if given the opportunities to do so.

As children become aware of writing around them and the use that others make of this writing, and as they see people engage in the act of writing, they appear to be learning three important things that are central to their own development as writers. Firstly they seem to become aware that writing is important, that it makes sense and that it has particular uses. Secondly they notice how writing makes sense. They become aware of the linguistic features of written language such as directionality and pattern. Finally they seem to realize that they too can communicate through written language. They can try out its uses and patterns and produce writing that communicates and looks like the models they see around them. There is now a great deal of support for this developmental model of learning about writing and learning to write and this is explored and summarized below.

A study of twenty-two five-year-olds in school by Dyson (1983) led her to propose a model of young children's writing development and learning about writing. She suggested that initially children seem to engage in writing simply for the satisfaction of doing so. At this stage they may produce lines of symbols that look like writing. Children who are at this stage are aware of writing but are not yet aware of how to convey meaning through writing.

During the next stage children may write letters and words but can not read these back. Even though their own writing does not necessarily convey a message they demonstrate that they know that writing can have meaning by asking others to read their writing to them. At this stage they are aware both of some of the features of written language and of its function to convey thoughts or information.

When children reach the third stage of writing they are going through the same processes as those used by adult writers. They decide on what they wish to communicate, call to mind the letter symbols needed to write that message and then write. Dyson suggests that children writing in this way go through two phases. First they produce and reproduce labels such as the names of familiar people and places and then after experimenting with labelling they progress to using writing for a variety of purposes and audiences.

Goodman (1990) has been analysing the writing of two- to six-year-old children over a period of twenty years. In the samples of writing that she has collected she has found children using writing in many different ways and she suggests that these represent some of the obvious uses of writing that children have noticed in the world around them. The spontaneous writing that children do at home, in the playgroup or at nursery school includes letters, invitations, lists, telephone messages, labels, notices and stories (Bissex, 1980; Goodman, 1990; Czerniewska, 1992). The significance of this is that children have learned that writing is a communicative activity undertaken for a particular reason and in the expectation that it will be read by others. It is clear that there are other sorts of writing, including using writing to clarify and organize thoughts, to explore ideas, to ask questions and for one's own enjoyment. It is also true that not all writing will be read by anyone other than the author. These ways of writing may not be immediately obvious to young children since their early experience of writing may largely have been that of seeing others read writing and witnessing or being asked to contribute to the writing of letters, cards and lists at home. But as children gain experience with using and seeing models of writing one might expect them to widen the ways in which they use writing.

Written language has a particular form which enables it to be understood and used and to communicate effectively between people. This form consists of features of the system that include letter shapes, directionality, spelling and punctuation. Studies of young children's writing have indicated that they are aware of the ways in which writing is organized so that it communicates effectively with its audience. Children's early writing reveals that, even before they have been taught to write, they seem to have an understanding of the organizing principles of written language and are actively engaged in exploring the system of writing. As children produce more writing and gain more experience of examining writing their writing shows increasing approximation to the linguistic principles used by fluent writers. These principles of written language are known as the recurring principle, the generative principle, the sign concept, the flexibility principle, and page and space arrangement principles (Clay, 1975; Temple *et al*, 1988).

The idea that writing consists of similar moves and shapes repeated over and over again is known as the recurring principle. Much of children's early representation of writing resembles lines of scribbles or contains rows of repeated shapes. Children will describe this as writing and know that it is different to pictures. As children repeat straight and curved lines in this way they are experimenting with the shapes that may become part of letter forms. In Figure 1.1, James, aged four, is practising making marks that resemble writing.

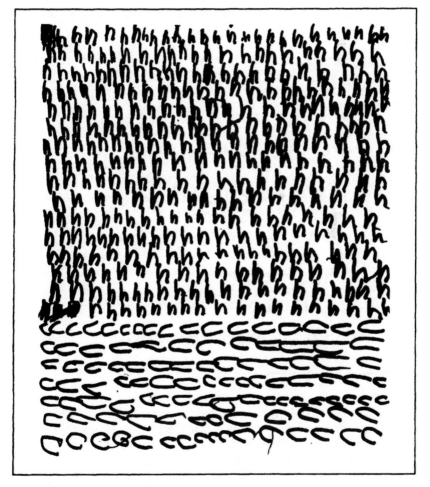

Figure 1.1

Written language consists of a set of symbols that can be combined in a variety of ways to produce words that are combined to produce meaning. Even though the set of characters is limited, a limitless amount of writing can be generated as long as the letters are combined in different ways. The idea that the same letters can be repeated in different combinations in writing is known as the generative principle.

In Figure 1.2, Sezer, aged five, shows his understanding of the generative principle by alternating and varying the letters he uses to produce a piece of writing. He uses and reuses the word *like* in order to generate a list of things he likes to eat. He has found a formula that enables him to communicate his thoughts in writing.

Figure 1.2

The sign concept in writing involves understanding that writing represents something other than itself. Amongst other things it can represent an idea, an object, a person or an opinion, but it is not the idea, the object, the person or the opinion. Writing represents meaning that may be recovered by the reader. When young children write they may first draw a picture and then write a series of symbols above, below or to the side of it. They will confidently identify one set of marks as the picture and another set of marks as the writing. They may go on to tell the onlooker what the writing 'says' or represents. Children who can do this understand the sign concept of writing. Figure 1.3 shows how Katie wrote her list of words, drew some of the items on the list and then read back her writing. She knew that writing conveys meaning, that it is different to pictures and that it may represent objects.

Figure 1.3

In their early writing children may often be observed to be testing the flexibility of the writing system. English writing is flexible in that it contains twenty-six letters that can be represented in a variety of upper- and lower-case scripts. For example, *a* may be written as A, **a** or *a*. It may also vary in size and decorative features. But there are limits to this flexibility. Although the twenty-six letters can be written in many different ways and styles, not all characters that include curved and straight lines are necessarily acceptable in the English language. An *h* is not an *h* if it is written with the curved shape to the left of the ascender or if it is written upside down. The discovery of what is and what is not acceptable in writing is known as the flexibility principle of writing. Figure 1.4 shows how Mary, aged four, was asked to show the teacher what she could write. She produced some recognizable letter shapes that she read back as *Mary*, *mummy* and *daddy*. However, she also included some numbers in her writing. She has not yet discovered the limits of the system. Similarly, children who reverse *b* and *d* in their writing are still experimenting with the flexibility principle.

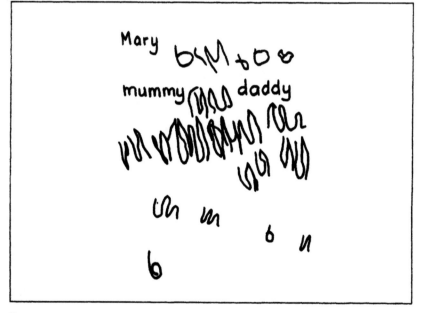

Figure 1.4

In many of the examples in this chapter it is possible to see that children are aware of the page arrangement principles of written language. They have produced writing that is arranged from left to right across the page and from top to bottom down the page. Sometimes young children forget this. Thomas, aged four, encountered problems when he ran out of room on his page and used the empty space above his initial writing to complete his sentence about going to the zoo. His first attempt at writing is contained within the box and he wrote his second attempt above this (Figure 1.5).

Figure 1.5

The preceding section has shown that young children are often familiar with the uses of writing and aware of some of the rules that govern written language. They are also willing to write and in doing so rehearse what they know about writing and make further discoveries about why and how writing is used.

Implications for teaching

It is now clear that many children have some understanding of the uses and forms of writing when they begin school. This has considerable implications for the way in which writing is organized and taught in school. One can not ignore what learners already know nor how they have learned about writing. It is important that the adults who teach children to write take account of what children already know, find ways of placing learning to write in a context that makes sense to them, motivate children to want to write, and enlarge their understanding of the purposes of writing.

It is no longer sufficient to begin the teaching of writing by asking the child to draw a picture, dictate a sentence about her picture to the teacher and then for the child to copy beneath the teacher's writing. This method of teaching draws attention to the limited parallels that exist between speaking and writing and takes little account of the wider communicative nature of writing or the distinctive power of writing. By placing the emphasis on copying, the adult is denying the child the opportunity to demonstrate what she already knows about writing and losing the opportunity to assess what the child can do and what needs to be taught next. If this type of task is repeated daily the teacher is ignoring the many purposes for which written language is often used and placing the emphasis on what the product looks like rather than on the process and use of writing. Rigid instructional settings and tasks that ignore and are incompatible with what children already know may limit rather than extend children's learning about writing since they do not necessarily match what the child is capable of and impede planning that caters for individual children's needs and that widens their understanding of writing.

In the past, teachers have felt that the difficulty of teaching writing to young children has been that when they start school they lack the ability to produce letters, words and sentences that can be read and understood. So before teaching children about the uses and composition of writing they have focused on the transcription elements of the writing system including letter formation, neatness, spelling and presentation. All children can produce marks on paper and have a go at writing but they know that they can not produce writing that looks like the teacher's writing. An overemphasis on the perfect presentation of writing from the beginning can inhibit children's willingness to write for themselves: they begin to feel that they can not write properly without copying and come to rely on the teacher for the writing that they do. By preventing children from producing their own writing and demonstrating their level of linguistic knowledge, teachers may undermine children's learning to date and deny themselves valuable opportunities to assess what children can do and direct their efforts into extending this.

When teachers work on the assumption that children often do have some knowledge about the form and function of print when they start school, they can spend their time encouraging children to produce their own writing. If children can produce a series of marks on a page and realize that marks on pages communicate meaning they have already learned some fundamental lessons about writing. This writing can then become a basis for discussion, and then learning and relevant teaching, linked to what the child can do, can begin. As the Programme of Study for English (DES, 1990) states, 'Initial efforts – marks on a page – will be followed by writing which is characterized by invented spelling and letter formation and partial understanding of many of the conventions of standard English.'

Teaching about writing proceeds slowly, sensitively and not always directly in the early stages of writing at school. It arises through experiences with print and the models that are presented to children. As Goodman (1986) wrote, 'Teachers who understand and respect the developmental aspects of writing in young children will organise instructional settings which build on and support the principles about writing which children have already developed . . . [they will] provide a rich learning environment which expands on what children already know.'

Just as oral language is learned in purposeful situations and in order to satisfy immediate goals set by the child, so the writing curriculum that is presented in school must engage children in purposeful writing activities. Whilst being relevant to the children the activities may also replicate the reasons for writing that adults use. It would be inappropriate to expect children to become interested and adept users of written language if they are not offered reasons for becoming so. Children can see real reasons for learning to speak; they communicate orally because they need to and want to. Adults need to explain, demonstrate and indicate by the writing tasks that are presented to children that writing is a useful way to communicate with others. What is common to all the forms of writing most often used by adults and imitated by children before they start school is that they have a purpose that is understood by the writer and an audience of whom the writer is aware.

The 1988 Assessment of Performance Unit (APU) survey of language performance revealed that 'not less than two out of ten pupils have developed negative views about writing by the time they are eleven'. The same report also stated that 'such attitudes are established long before pupils reach the age of eleven. It can be assumed that they are established primarily when children are first being taught to read and write' (Gorman et al., 1989). During the course of the National Writing Project (1989) children were asked why they wrote and many of the children's responses showed that they were not at all clear about the purposes of writing. They gave replies such as 'teacher says so' and 'so we don't get told off'.

Learners rarely sustain interest in an activity that has little meaning for them. Children's early learning is undertaken with a purpose that is relevant to the child. Whitehead (1990) explains that children seem to ask themselves two questions when engaging in a task: first, 'What is it for?' and second, 'What's in it for me?' It is important that answers to both these questions are provided for children if they are to produce their best when writing and if they are to sustain their interest in writing over time. If, as the APU survey suggests, negative attitudes to writing begin at the start of a child's school career and if children learn most effectively when they can see reasons for what they are learning, then it might be important both to present children with writing activities that have a purpose and to make these purposes explicit and relevant to young children in order to motivate them as writers.

Writing has a range of uses, it can be addressed to oneself or to others and it can be written in a variety of styles. It is important, wherever possible, to replicate this understanding of purpose, audience and style in the classroom. The writing curriculum at school can cover all the purposes for which writing is used as children write stories, personal journals, poems, letters, responses, questions, invitations, explanations, labels, notices, adverts, posters, reviews, scripts, jokes, accounts and talks. However, it is not sufficient just to provide a range of writing activities; it is also necessary to provide real audiences for children's writing wherever possible. If the only audience for writing in the classroom is the teacher and there is no indication of what will happen to the writing when it is finished other than that it will be corrected, children will not see writing as a useful communicative act and there may be little motivation for them to write well and interestingly. Writing at school should cover the range of writing uses that exists and each piece of writing that is done should be set in its context so that content, style and presentation are also varied and suited to the audience. As children gain experience as writers, writing for different purposes and audiences, adults will be able to show them how to make choices about what they write and the words that they use. They will be able to introduce children to the idea that control over words, the ability to manipulate meaning and to select words from a vast repertoire, is a powerful method of communication.

Conclusion

If children are to learn to write easily and willingly, the adults who teach them need to consider what writing is for, how it is used and its distinctive features as a system of communication. They need to discover what children know about the functional and linguistic features of writing when they start school and to appreciate how children have learned what they have. If adults are aware of the uses of writing and children's understanding of writing, they can then formulate an approach to writing that supports rather than negates children's early learning about literacy, that encourages children to explore how written language works and that enables children to recognize the uses that writing has for them.

2

Writing at School

Introduction

This chapter examines approaches to writing at school. Practice varies
widely and the particular method of teaching may be linked to teachers'
perceptions of what writing is and what writing is for. The thrust of the
argument in this chapter is that developmental writing most closely
matches our current understanding of what writing is, how it is learned
and what it is used for. The first section, 'How it used to be', documents
traditional methods of teaching children to write and the problems that
may arise when teaching writing in these ways. These problems include
what children learn about writing and organizational difficulties for the
teacher. It also describes how these concerns have led practitioners to
look for new ways of teaching writing. The second section provides an
overview of developmental writing and includes some suggestions for
those who wish to change or extend their approach to writing. The third
section, 'Stages of developmental writing', gives examples of children's
writing gathered from schools using a developmental approach. These
show how children develop as writers. Each example is accompanied by
a commentary which indicates how teachers can extend and support
children as writers when they work with what children can do.

How it used to be

The investigations into literacy that have taken place during the past
decade have enabled practitioners and researchers to appreciate more
clearly the form and function of writing and to acknowledge young
children's awareness of writing when they begin school. Prior to this,
approaches to the teaching of writing in school usually began from the
premise that children started school with little or no knowledge about
writing and how to write. It was thought that children could only learn to

write after receiving formal instruction from the teacher. It was assumed that independent writing was the last stage to be reached and that it followed a programme that included writing over the teacher's writing, tracing over the teacher's writing, copying underneath the teacher's writing and copying from the board. When children began to write alone they were usually given word books and encouraged to take care with their spelling and handwriting. Very often the task that was given to the class was to write their news or to produce a story, an account or a description. The children rarely received an explanation of why they were writing, who was going to read the writing and what would happen to the writing once it was finished. Often the only reason for writing was to gain practice at writing and the only audience for the writing was the teacher. After the piece of writing was finished it was corrected by the teacher and remained in the child's writing book. Later it might be shown to parents as evidence of the child's achievement and progress in writing. This approach made it difficult for the teacher to see what children could do alone, did not convey the purposes of writing to children, put the emphasis on transcription rather than composition and failed to give children a sense of the communicative or personal uses of writing.

This method of teaching children to write has been questioned by many teachers. They have seen that working in this way has many disadvantages. Copying and asking for words encourages children to become reliant on the teacher and often accounts for the lines of children that follow the teacher around the classroom with their word books open, or for the numbers of children sitting at their tables with their hands up waiting for the teacher to write their sentence in their 'news books'. Teachers have seen that a great deal of time can be wasted by children as they wait for help and that when the teacher gives the required assistance she is generally helping children with getting the writing to look right rather than responding to what the children have written and looking at ways to develop this. Whilst asking children to produce exciting, interesting, detailed and well-constructed pieces of writing, many teachers realized that they could spend much of their time in writing sessions not helping with any of these aspects of writing.

For many years people have been conscious of the poor attitudes to writing that many children develop (Gorman et al., 1989). Poor attitudes to writing may arise for many reasons, but the way that writing is taught and the messages that the teacher transmits about writing will influence children's feelings about writing and their view of themselves as writers. Children may think that they have nothing to say that needs to be communicated through writing. They may feel that the demands that are placed on them to produce neat, correctly spelt writing at the first attempt are difficult to meet. Children may feel that their writing is not very good, that they are poor spellers and that their handwriting looks untidy even if the content is fine, and this may lead them to become discouraged with what they write. They may feel that writing takes too long if they have to wait for every spelling from the teacher or for the teacher to write their sentence down before they copy it. Writing sessions may not occur regularly enough for children to spend time on one piece until they have something that is worth reading by others. Alternatively, writing may happen too often, with everything that happens in the class being followed by an exhortation by the teacher to write about it. Writing in the class may be organized so that children do not see the purpose of it, they may feel that only the teacher reads what they write. Finally, even if the child has something to write about and someone to write for, if it is the transcription rather than the content that is attended to first by the teacher, the child may assume that the message is unimportant. In the long term, asking children to write with the emphasis on transcription and without any clear sense of purpose and audience negates the communicative function of writing and is likely to alienate children from wanting to write at school and at home.

We have become much more aware of the fact that writers write because they have something to communicate and someone to communicate with or because they have something to remember or clarify. They do not write if what they write can more easily and just as successfully be spoken. Children can very often tell elaborate stories or pieces of news at school but when it comes to putting this down on paper they produce one sentence. This might be because they can see no advantage in communicating this information again through writing. They have already communicated with a wider audience than their writing will reach, and writing their story down will involve them in the chore of wrestling with transcription. They may well wonder what advantage is to be gained from writing at school.

In spite of the disadvantages with traditional approaches to writing, in terms of what it is that teachers are teaching and what it is that children are learning, many schools have continued to teach writing in this way. Many teachers still feel obliged to spend a great deal of time on getting children to copy what they write either in the child's writing book or in their word books. There may be a number of reasons for this. Traditionally teachers seem to have felt that writing that has been displayed in school or that has been available for parents to read on open evenings should either look perfect or should show evidence of having been corrected. Teachers seem to think that if all the mistakes made by a child are not attended to parents will assume that they are failing to teach. However, in reality parents, like teachers, know that their children can not write perfectly on their own just as teachers know that even though children can copy writing perfectly they can rarely write as well without the teacher's help. No one is fooled by perfect examples of children's writing. When parents see perfectly presented writing on displays they are often looking at children's copies of the teacher's writing and the corrections they see in children's books are more likely to be evidence of the teacher's industry than of the child's learning. As people have begun to question this approach to writing they have concluded that by teaching in a way that is based on copying, teachers may be reinforcing parental expectations about what they will see in school, rather than helping children to become writers.

Developmental writing

As our understanding of how children learn and how children learn about writing has changed so the approach to writing in school has also begun to change. Increasingly children are being viewed as active learners who take initiatives in their own learning both outside and inside school. As a result teachers have begun to use teaching strategies that take account of what children already know and work from what children can do.

Children learn to become language users by abstracting, hypothesizing, constructing and revising knowledge about the language system (Bissex, 1984). By the time they start school they have abstracted a great deal of knowledge about the writing system from the examples they have seen around them; they may have hypothesized about what it is for and how it works. When they begin to write they are constructing writing based on their abstractions and hypotheses about the system. When they begin school most children are in a position to construct or represent what they have learned so far about writing.

Teachers who have a developmental approach to writing accept that when young children start school they have a great deal of knowledge about writing, knowledge that has been learned from the literate world that surrounds them. Children understand that symbols in books, on advertising hoardings and in newspapers carry meaning and that this representation of meaning is called writing. Teachers also acknowledge that the formal process of learning to write begins when the child first makes marks on a page and says, 'I'm writing'. When children start school the majority of them believe they can write. Given enough preschool experience with drawing and writing materials, they will have begun to integrate letter-like symbols into their drawings and paintings. Writing begins to emerge from experimenting with symbols, letters, numbers, strings of letters and early attempts at words. If children are given a great deal of exposure to print of all types and if they are read to frequently, they will begin to extract detail and meaning from print and start to create it for themselves in their own attempts at writing. Teachers who work developmentally work with what children bring to school in terms of knowledge about writing and the ability to write, rather than seeing learning to write as something that is imposed from without. Within the classroom children are expected to try and write themselves. They are given the opportunity to 'have a go' at writing without copying or waiting for the teacher to help them with spellings before they write. Initially children are encouraged to write without worrying about spelling and handwriting. They are given a purposeful task that focuses on one of the many uses of writing and, wherever possible, an audience other than the teacher is provided for the writing that they do. The teacher provides encouragement and support as the children write. She encourages children to discuss their writing, to think about their writing and to think about how things should be written. The children are expected to think about what writing looks like and how they can best represent meaning and ideas in print. Children are asked to engage actively with the process of writing. The teacher works with what is constructed and with what children know in order to revise and extend children's understanding of writing. It is after the writing has been produced that the teacher gives the children feedback and help with the transcriptional elements of what has been written. In this way teachers take away the emphasis on spelling and place it on composition, structure, clarity and meaning. Such teachers build upon and extend what children can do and through observation and sensitive intervention help them to write more fluently and more easily. This approach to teaching and learning that links the unknown to the known and relies on intervention rather than imposition is known as developmental.

To retain confidence in their ability to write, children need opportunities to write meaningfully, to discuss their writing and to try out writing in a way that an experienced writer would. Routine, meaningless writing at school can sap confidence and lead to a dependent, boring output. To encourage the development of good, meaningful writing, children must be exposed to good models, which include books in class and at home, print used for a purpose and the sight of experienced writers working. Developmental writing can not be carried on in isolation. It needs the support of exposure to print and the experience of seeing writers at work so that children can extend their understanding of the purpose and process of writing, consider the way that written symbols work and begin to integrate such knowledge into their own attempts.

The process of learning to write is not quick. It takes time for children to progress through all the stages of learning about writing and learning how to write, moving from marks on a page to fluent writing. However, it is important that children are given the time to experiment with each stage of the writing process if they are to discover the range of writing that is available and the way that the writing system is organized. What-ever stage children have reached they need to feel that their written efforts are valuable if they are to continue to write and to develop positive attitudes to writing. The teacher does not correct every error that the child makes when writing; instead she provides correct models for the child to see and works on one or two mistakes or difficulties at a time.

Expressing what is meant through the written word can be both time-consuming and hard work. Writing is also an idiosyncratic process and success and involvement with writing can vary from task to task and from day to day. There are three important elements of designing a writing curriculum for children: firstly, that they are given tasks that involve real reasons to communicate meaning through writing; sec-ondly, that they are initially given time to work on a piece of writing and time to return to it later either alone or with the teacher's help; and, thirdly, that they have opportunities to write in different styles and with different degrees of concentration depending on the task.

Developmental writing is not just about the choice and use of resources and the selection of activities that take note of a variety of purposes and audiences for writing. It is principally about an understanding of how writing develops, an understanding of how children learn to write in the context of how children learn. This understanding is central for the teacher since it is around this that she makes decisions about when and how to intervene in order to develop each child's writing ability. The organization of resources and activities provides the setting within which each child can experiment with writing and demonstrate what she has learnt about writing and within which the teacher works to extend each child's achievement.

A developmental approach to writing offers learners and teachers many advantages since it fosters:

- children's confidence to believe in themselves as writers from the outset since the teacher accepts the knowledge and understanding that children have and teaches from this;
- children who are active participants in their own writing develop-ment;
- learners who are willing to take a chance and to risk being wrong;
- independence from the start since it encourages children to puzzle out things for themselves;

- smooth classroom organization since it aims to remove dependence on the teacher for all that is written;
- a positive attitude towards writing and a desire to communicate in the written form, since children may see that writing is easier than they think if the teacher is not in the first instance overly concerned with correct letter formation, correct spelling and neatness;
- the strategies to enable the child to complete a whole piece of writing;
- the message that writing is primarily about communication of content;
- opportunities to discover the ways in which writing is used;
- a better understanding of spelling because children are asked to think about how words look and how to represent these in their writing so that the reader can understand them.

Getting started

For those who are not used to developmental writing but who feel that they would like to change their current practice and make a start on developmental writing it may be difficult to know where to begin. It may feel as though all the structures that one normally uses have been taken away. Developmental writing does not mean telling the class that they are never to use a spelling book or dictionary again and that they can write what they want, how they want. Instead it needs to be introduced thoughtfully and systematically. Listed below are a number of pointers that may help those who are considering introducing developmental writing to their pupils.

1 Observe and consider in depth what the children are doing at present when they write.
2 Make a list of the good and bad features of current practice.
3 Find out more about developmental writing and compare this with what has been discovered through observation of the class at work.
4 Think about the changes to organization, resources, timing and activities that will be necessary if a developmental approach is to work.
5 When you feel confident about what you want to achieve, have enough knowledge and enough support within the school, you are ready to begin.
6 Explain to the children what this new approach involves.
7 Gradually remove word books from the children.
8 Begin to encourage developmental writing with groups of children in the class. Encourage them to 'have a go' at writing on their own whilst ensuring that they can read back what they have written. Accept their early attempts at writing and take time to reassure them and to praise their unaided efforts.

9 Continue this until developmental writing is standard practice in the class.

10 Analyse the writing carefully to see what children can do and what they know about writing. It is soon easy to see where children are with print and how adult intervention will help them to learn more.

11 Formulate and implement a varied writing curriculum in the class with tasks that take account of purpose and audience.

12 Give the process time. Don't expect results immediately. Developmental writing, as with any innovation, cannot be introduced quickly or half-heartedly. A gradual, informed and enthusiastic introduction is always best and inspires children with confidence.

Stages of developmental writing

This section examines the various stages of developmental writing and suggests strategies for helping children to move on. The work was collected from children who demonstrate a wide range of abilities and was undertaken in a number of different schools in rural and urban locations. The writing was produced in a variety of contexts, including mathematics, science and English, and on the child's initiative as well as in response to the teacher's suggestions. The samples are arranged to show progress in writing and indicate the features that adults might expect to see as children gain more experience in writing. The samples are not intended to represent the 'best' that each age group can achieve, rather examples have been included that show common errors as these may be points that teachers or adults wish to work on with children. Each piece of writing is discussed under three headings: 'Context', 'Comment' and 'What next?' The 'Context' gives some information about the child and the circumstances surrounding the production of the writing. The 'Comment' section indicates what each writer has achieved and what is presenting difficulties. I have included the level of attainment demonstrated by the child in this particular piece of writing in this section since teachers may find this helpful. However, I do recognize that more writing samples would be needed before a firm assessment of attainment in writing could be made since levels are assigned to children's capabilities as demonstrated through a range of samples produced for a range of purposes, not single pieces of writing. The 'What next?' section makes some practical suggestions about how teachers can assist children's development as writers.

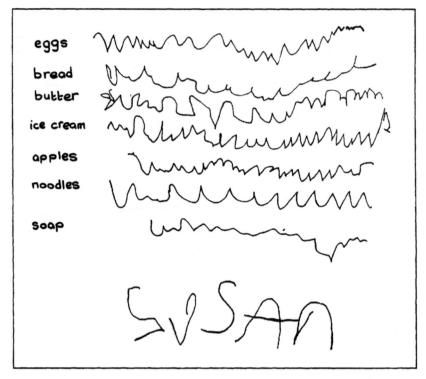

eggs

bread

butter

ice cream

apples

noodles

soap

Figure 2.1

Susan aged four (Figure 2.1)

Context
Susan chose to do this writing alone in the writing area. She showed her writing to the teacher and read it to her. The teacher wrote out the items on the shopping list next to Susan's writing.

Comment
By choosing to write, Susan indicated that she felt confident and positive about writing. The piece of writing takes the form of left-to-right scribble arranged in the form of a list. It shows that the child is aware of the direction of writing in English and of page arrangement principles. As Susan was writing across the page she was practising some of the shapes that may be incorporated into letters that will comprise her writing at a later date. Susan is clear about the distinction between writing and drawing and is moving towards level one of the statements of attainment for writing.

What next?

The teacher should continue to encourage Susan to write during both play activities and writing sessions. A range of writing materials should help to maintain Susan's interest in writing. The teacher might begin to draw Susan's attention to the letters that are found in her name and begin to discuss how letters combine to produce words. Discussion of text in books will also draw Susan's attention to the details of writing.

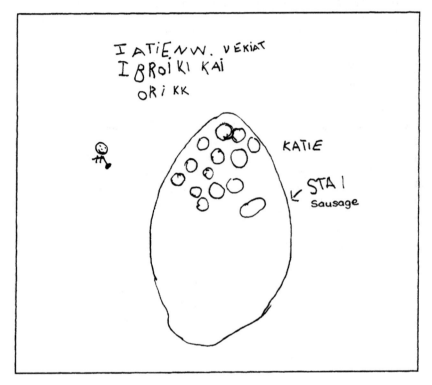

Figure 2.2

Katie, aged four (Figure 2.2)

Context

The class was working on the theme of food and the children had been asked to draw and write about their favourite food. The writing that the children produced was going to be incorporated into a class book of favourite foods. Katie produced this writing and drawing unaided. After Katie finished her writing the teacher wrote the word *sausage* under Katie's word *STAI*.

Comment

Katie approached this writing with confidence. After writing about the baked beans, Katie decided that sausages were also her favourite food and drew a sausage shape around her drawing of the beans, writing *STAI* for sausage with an arrow pointing to the shape. In this piece of writing Katie demonstrates that she can spell her name, knows a number of letter forms and knows some initial sounds. She combines the letters from her name to represent a number of words. She was able to read back her writing and identified the *B* as the initial letter of *baked beans*. Katie is aware of the need to leave spaces between words and arranges her writing from left to right and top to bottom on the page. In this piece of writing the writing, spelling and handwriting would be assessed at level 1.

What next?

The teacher might write the translation of Katie's sentence underneath her writing, thus presenting Katie with a model of lower-case writing. She would praise Katie's use of initial sounds. The teacher might draw Katie's attention to the spelling of the word *like*, showing her how it includes some of the letters from her name. Katie needs to continue writing for a variety of purposes and to experiment with writing. With continued practice she should continue to make good progress.

Figure 2.3

Kurt, aged five (Figure 2.3)

Context

The children were working on aspects of time and had been asked to think of things that they did at various parts of the day. This sentence represents Kurt's answer to the question, 'What do you do after school?'

Comment

Kurt wrote this very quickly and with confidence. Although only *I* and *Kurt* are spelt correctly, it is easy to make sense of what he has written. The spelling of *bed* is very close to conventional spelling and he uses initial letter sounds to begin each word. This piece of work would fulfil the statements of attainment at level 1 for writing, spelling and handwriting.

What next?

The teacher could write out in full what Kurt has written to provide him with a model of writing and to draw his attention to the similarities as well as the differences between his writing and her writing. She might discuss his reversal of the letter *d*. Kurt is making good progress at writing. He would benefit from undertaking longer pieces of writing and from writing tasks that challenge him to think about his audience. Kurt's writing ability will develop as he gains more practice at writing and as he reads books with adults.

Onec upon a time there was a blatck and white raBbit his name was niBBallS.

Figure 2.4

Suraj, aged six (Figure 2.4)

Context

Suraj was writing a book to be included in the class library. This was the first page of his first draft in the story of Nibbles.

Comment

Suraj is very clear about how stories begin. He uses a conventional story opening and then introduces his central character. He has described the rabbit and given it a name. He has begun to self-correct his writing and has experimented with spelling *once* although it is still not clear that it is correct. He is drawing on visual and phonic cues for spelling. He is also beginning to use punctuation although he has not used a capital letter for the name of the rabbit. This writing indicates that Suraj is likely to reach the level 2 statements of attainment for writing and spelling but needs to use lower-case letters more consistently before he can attain level 2 for handwriting.

What next?
The teacher would praise Suraj for what he has written so far and encourage him to complete his book. She would also commend him for proofreading his writing. She might encourage Suraj to describe his rabbit more fully and encourage him to incorporate detail into his writing. She might also point out to Suraj that he could find the correct spelling for *once* in one of the books in the reading corner. She might talk to Suraj about his use of upper-case letters in the middle of words. As Suraj forms his letters well and some letters show baseline joining strokes, the teacher might begin to introduce Suraj to cursive script. This may help to eliminate the reversals in his writing.

Melanie, aged six (Figure 2.5)
My dog is black and very fast when she runs. When my mum comes in my dog snaps at her because she thinks its someone to play with. My dog is a lurcher and a playful one too.

Context
This piece of writing was undertaken as part of the work on the theme of pets. It was to be incorporated into a class book. Melanie had been asked to think about the ideas she wished to include in the piece of writing before she wrote her first draft. She planned her ideas by making a list before she wrote her description.

Comment
This piece of writing is clearly organized, contains detail about the dog, and the final sentence forms an excellent conclusion to the writing. Melanie uses full stops appropriately and her conclusion has the appearance of a final paragraph, although this may have been unconscious. For her first draft Melanie has not lingered over words that she can not spell but has concentrated on content and organization. Melanie is clearly reaching level 2 in the statements of attainment for writing, spelling and handwriting.

1 Blak
2 I ucha
3 {that t erad
4 very frst.
5 snapy ✓
6 plafall ✓

my doG is Blak
and very frst when
my mum cums in my
dog snaps at ha becas
she tiks its sum whn to
play with.
my dog is a lucha
and a plafall wun too.

Figure 2.5

What next?
After writing her first draft Melanie should be encouraged to read
through her work and correct or identify any mistakes. She could be
encouraged to find common words that she has misspelt in dictionaries
or in other books in the classroom. In this particular piece of work the
teacher might work with Melanie on the spelling of *some* and *come*, using
the 'look, cover, remember, write, check' method.

George Kinrade.

october 13th 1992.

My book review

Almost goodbye Guzzler.
By Helen cresswell and Judy brown.
Once there was a little boy whos
teacher said lets have a white
elephant stall. So guzzler went
to an old ladys house and she
gave him a lamp. He rubbed the
lamp and out came a genie he
wished he was invisible.
I liked the book because it was
very very funny it has black and
white illustrations. The books
illustrations are set out like a
cartoons pictures. I liked the book
because it is funny and It made
me laugh a lot. The pictures go
with the words. I think the book would
be suitable for 7 to 9 year olds.
Alomst goodbye guzzler get it on your
shelf now.

Figure 2.6

George, aged seven (Figure 2.6)

Context
This was a book review written for display in the book corner. This was a second draft. The first draft was written quickly and the handwriting was untidy; it had also contained a number of misspellings. After writing the first draft George had used a dictionary and the book itself to correct his spelling before rewriting the review using a felt-tip pen.

Comment
This piece of writing is clearly structured and well organized. George distinguishes between his summary of the book and his reaction to the book by using two sections or paragraphs. His ending demonstrates that he is aware of his audience and the purpose of the writing. In terms of content and presentation this is an excellent piece of work. This piece of writing indicates that George has reached levels 3a, 3d and 3e of the statements of attainment for writing, levels 3a, 3b and 3d in the statements of attainment for spelling, and levels 2a and 2b in the statements of attainment for handwriting.

What next?
George is a competent writer with a good sense of how and what to write. The teacher might begin to extend George's presentation skills. He has used one apostrophe correctly in *book's* and would seem to be ready to learn about the use of the apostrophe and speech marks. As all his letters are correctly formed it would now be a good time to introduce George to cursive script and this should help him to write more quickly and fluently.

Kevin aged eight (Figure 2.7)

Context
The class had had a discussion about valentines. They were then asked to write about their valentine and this writing was to be enclosed in a valentine card that they could give to the person they had written about. This was a first draft but the children were told to take care with it as it would be read by the person of their choice.

Comment
Kevin has produced a humorous tribute to his family. He has used the conventions of language to good effect, including dramatic pauses and self-depreciating humour. He has given the reasons for his choice of valentines and his description of Pippin is at once caring and detailed. As a piece of writing this has many strengths and Kevin has taken care

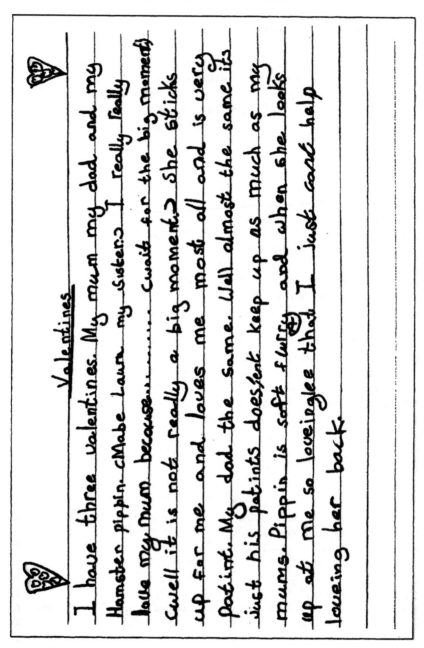

<u>Valentines</u>

I have three valentines. My mum my dad and my
Hamster pippin. CMabe Laura my sister. I really really
love my mum because.......... Cwait for the big moment
Cwell it is not really a big moment. she sticks
up for me and loves me most all and is very
patint. My dad the same. Well almost the same its
just his patints doestent keep up as much as my
mums. Pippin is soft fluffy and when she looks
up at me so loveinglee that I just cant help
loveing her back.

Figure 2.7

with it. If Kevin were encouraged to read his writing through again he would see that he has omitted some words; he has also produced some good phonic misspellings. Kevin is clearly an able writer and this piece of writing shows him to be reaching some of the level 3 statements of attainment for writing, some of the level 3 statements of attainment for spelling and the level 2 statements of attainment for handwriting.

What next?
In the future the teacher might introduce Kevin to the skill of proofreading. She might work with Kevin on developing visual strategies when spelling and on the use of dictionaries and other sources of spelling help. Some of Kevin's writing is joined and the teacher might begin to help him join letters more consistently. He uses punctuation well and it seems as if he is ready to be introduced to more sophisticated uses of punctuation such as the apostrophe.

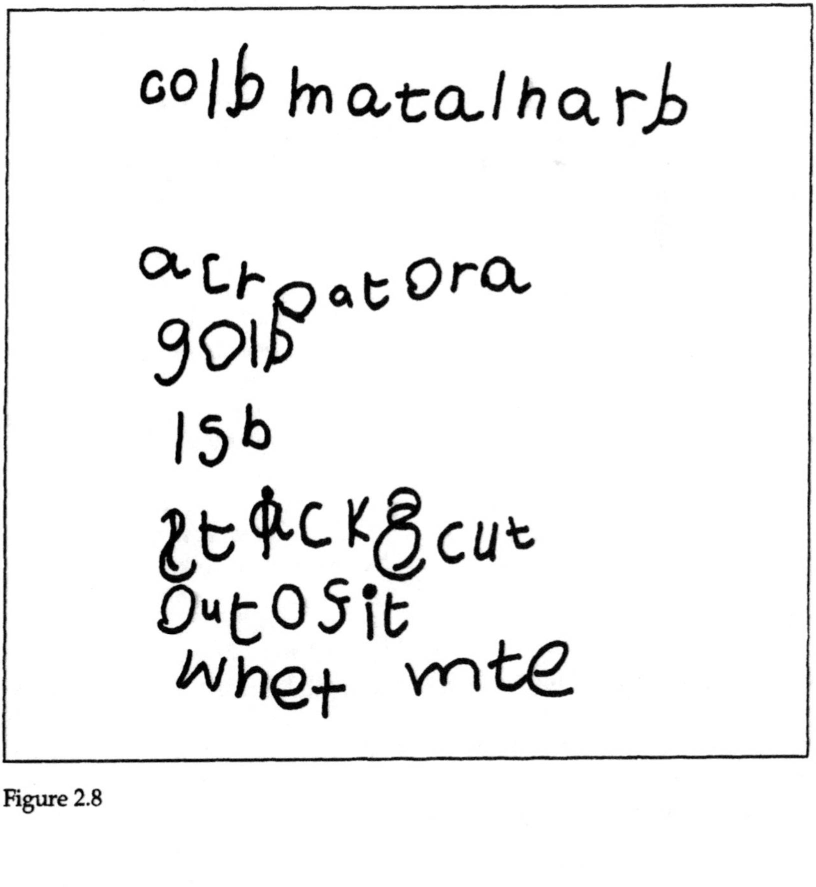

Figure 2.8

James aged six (Figure 2.8)
This piece of writing by James was his first attempt at developmental writing. I was told that James could not write anything except by copying beneath the teacher's writing. I asked James to 'have a go' at writing something to describe a brass ornamental snail that his group was writing about. He wrote this without any help. It reads:

cold metal hard
a creature
gold
eyes
sticks cut
out of it
white metal

Clearly James could write on his own when given the opportunity and the encouragement.

Conclusion

Developmental writing takes account of general theories about learning and theories about learning to write and can lead to efficient and effective classroom practice. If teachers' use of a developmental approach to writing is to be effective they need to know what children are likely to be able to do and why they do it at each stage of their growth in writing experience and ability. Such an awareness helps when making judgements about what intervention is appropriate at each stage. Reference to a theory or a model makes it easier to identify what might come next and thus enables practitioners to devise strategies that enable them to guide pupils on to the next stage and ensure progression. Working from what children do achieve in writing helps one to assess positively and to see the tremendous amount of learning children display at each stage of development. Teaching is important within a developmental framework since it exists to move the learner on from one stage to the next and helps the children to learn the skills, concepts and attitudes that are necessary if they are to achieve success in all aspects of writing.

Questions about writing at school

Q.   When helping a child with developmental writing, how do I know what to correct?
A.   Each piece of work requires individual assessment. But as a general rule no more than two or three errors should be given attention. If the child can identify corrections that she would like to make, these can be a

good starting point for the teacher. If not, you can select what seems to be most appropriate to the child's needs and the situation from content, structure, spelling, handwriting or presentation. It is often most useful to concentrate on the things that the child has almost got right or corrections that apply not only to this particular piece of writing but that will be used again. These are more likely to be remembered.

Q. What does the teacher or adult do when the child can not read anything she has written?

A. This can be a perfectly normal stage in the development of writing competence and there are two ways in which the teacher can respond. Firstly, if this is free writing there is no need to do anything except perhaps to praise the child for wishing to produce some writing on her own initiative and for any similarities to adult writing that it might contain. Secondly, if you have a rough idea of the content, write what you and the child agree might have been the message beneath the child's writing. This provides a model of writing for the child to emulate. This modelling process may need to continue for some time, but every time the child sees an adult write she is learning some valuable points about writing.

Q. What do I do with the child who says, 'I can't write'?

A. Very few children are unable to have a go at writing; what they may really be saying is that they can not write in the same way as an experienced writer or produce writing that looks like that seen in books. It may be necessary for you to spend some time explaining that you do not expect to see perfect writing but that you will be pleased with whatever the child writes. The teacher's role will be to encourage and gently insist that the child tries. Sometimes, in order to foster the child's confidence and to get her started, the teacher or adult may begin the child's writing and ask the child to write the next word or to help with spelling some of the words. The adult and the child can collaborate on the writing while the teacher builds up the child's confidence. Usually, once the child sees the rest of the class writing unaided she will want to join in and write in the same way as her peers.

3

Writing in Practice

Introduction

This chapter looks at practical ways to support developmental writing in the classroom. It examines the teacher's role in supporting children's learning and in organizing for writing. The teacher is responsible for the management and organization of learning in the classroom and for creating a positive learning atmosphere that supports her teaching and the children's learning. The second and third sections contain suggestions about resources and activities that are helpful when introducing children to the way in which writing is used and the way that writers write in the world outside school. These should enable practitioners to plan an effective and meaningful writing curriculum for early-years pupils.

The role of the teacher

The teacher has a fourfold role as she teaches writing developmentally. She acts as a facilitator, a model, an adviser and an observer, as she plans, teaches and refines the writing curriculum and as she extends the writing abilities of the pupils.

As a facilitator the teacher provides the resources that children need when they write. She makes sure that there is a varied and sufficient stock of writing materials available. Other resources that can support children's independent writing, such as alphabet friezes, collections of words and dictionaries, should also be present for the children to use. The teacher thinks about designing a classroom that is a literate environment with a writing corner, displays of writing, and a well-stocked library area. As a facilitator the teacher is responsible for planning writing tasks that are purposeful, varied and interesting and for ensuring that the writing produced is valued and displayed. As well as organizing resources and activities the teacher may organize other adults in the classroom to work alongside children as scribes, to operate the computer keyboard or in other ways that enable children to witness how writing is constructed and allow them to compose at greater length than they could if they were writing on their own.

The teacher demonstrates what writers do through her attitude to writing, her own writing in the classroom and in shared-writing sessions with the children. She may want to demonstrate to children her own use of a dictionary and she may draw children's attention to textual features of writing when reading stories and sharing big books with the class. When the opportunity arises the teacher will explain to the children about the function of the writing that she engages in the classroom. Situations such as taking the register, writing for displays and writing letters and notes provide these opportunities. Through the examples of writing she provides she sets the standard for writing that she expects the class to aim for.

When working as an adviser the teacher works with the pupils on their writing. In the early stages of writing she may be encouraging children to have a go at writing, to focus on what words look like or what letter words begin with. She may write the correctly transcribed version of what the child has written beneath the child's writing and discuss this with her. As the child progresses in confidence and competence she may teach specific skills such as letter formation or strategies for spelling correctly such as 'look, cover, remember, write, check' or how to use word banks and dictionaries. Later she may demonstrate strategies such as drafting and revising. The teacher may advise on various ways of representing written responses such as using lists and diagrams as alternatives to prose. She will also be making suggestions on how to improve the content, organization and vocabulary in writing. At times she will be praising what children produce and looking for ways to enhance achievement.

Finally, the teacher acts as an observer of children as they write. As she monitors the children and their work she considers how successful she has been as a facilitator. Would the children benefit more from different tasks? Do they need more or different resources? She considers her role as a model. Is this sufficient for the children's development, or do they perhaps need more shared-writing sessions? She also thinks about when she should intervene and how to intervene to support each child's writing development. The National Curriculum Council's non-statutory guidance for writing states that the 'effective teaching of writing depends upon the ability of the teacher to identify when the child needs support and advice in order to make further progress' (NCC, 1989). In the light of her observations she can then change aspects of her teaching as it is manifested through any of her roles in the classroom.

Classroom organization

It is easier to help children with their writing if only a small group of children are writing at one time. It is difficult for the teacher to provide effective teaching if she is dealing with thirty writers at once. Daily organization needs to take account of this. A classroom where groups of children are engaged on a mix of activities that demand different degrees of attention from the teacher will put less pressure on the teacher as she responds to children's learning needs. A typical classroom scene might reveal one group of children making a circuit with bulbs, wires and batteries, another group may be making a large model of a house which will be lit by the circuits, another group may be illustrating a book about their homes that they have just finished writing, a fourth group might be writing a first draft of an information text about their homes, and the final group of children might be engaged in a mathematics task involving measuring models of their homes and recording the results. The science and technology activities currently under way in the classroom may be the starting point for the next writing activity for these groups of children when they write about what they did, what they needed and what they found out as they completed their tasks. The writing and the illustrating activities may be part of the preparation for the model building; they may be helping the children to plan how they will go about practical tasks. The children who are measuring and recording are also writing. Other follow-up activities to writing may include making a book and designing a cover for the book. Not all these activities will demand the same degree of attention from the teacher. Planning a range of activities that demand different degrees of teacher attention can give the teacher more time to spend on productive intervention with the children who are writing.

Children who are writing do not always need to write alone. The teacher may ask children to work in pairs to compose and write, using each other as sources of ideas and help with writing. This again helps the teacher to use her time more effectively as she can work with two children at once when she checks on their progress or, if the children are providing effective help for one another, she can let them get on alone and spend time with other children in the class.

If the writing that is done in school is to mirror the way writers write in the world outside school the children will plan, draft, revise and publish many of the pieces of writing that they produce. All this takes time and not all children will finish each stage at the same time. Within a group of writers there may be children who are planning and some who are making a final copy of their writing. The teacher can expect children to carry on with a piece of writing over the course of a few days when they are involved with what they are doing. Again this helps to take pressure off the teacher since at the final draft stage she will not be needed by the children and will be able to concentrate on working with those pupils who are planning or revising their work.

The organization of writing will never be fixed or static and will vary according to the activity, but when children are used to working independently and to thinking about their work there is less demand on the teacher for fragmented help with individual spellings and more time for the teacher to give help on all aspects of writing, including content, structure and style as well as spelling and handwriting, at the appropriate time.

Above all, the teacher is responsible for the general learning ethos in her classroom and with the children she teaches. It is important that the classroom climate is one where risk-taking is encouraged rather than discouraged. It is impossible to learn without making mistakes. Mistakes are rarely a problem but usually present opportunities for learning. Learning need not be competitive or individual. Instead, learning at school should be regarded as a collaborative enterprise between the teacher and her pupils and between the pupils themselves. All classroom activities should encourage the pupils to share what they know with others and to listen to the ideas that others offer to them. If schools and classes work in this way they may become true communities of learners.

The classroom as a writing environment

A well-planned and well-resourced classroom offers children many models of writing and the opportunity to practise writing in a variety of ways as well as promoting a positive image of writing to the children. It is likely that children will respond positively to writing if it is given a high profile in the classroom and it is clear that the teacher values writing.

The writing area

In general, classrooms contain many resources that promote children's writing development. Such resources include books, alphabet friezes, wooden, plastic, velvet and magnetic letters, paper and writing implements. It is often helpful if these are generally available and stored in one part of the classroom that is known as the writing area. This can then become a focal point for writing and writing resources in the classroom. An attractive and well-resourced writing area transmits the message that writing is important and worth while and signifies its status to the class. Practicalities, such as the size of the classroom, influence the amount of space that can be given to the area, determine whether the area is used for writing and how many children can work there at one time.

The writing area should contain all the resources that children need to write. Children can choose either to work in this area or they can collect the resources and materials they need for writing from it. Resources in the writing area might include:

- a variety of different sizes, shapes, colours and quality of paper including scrap paper;
- card;
- coupons and forms to fill in;
- envelopes;
- postcards and greeting cards representing a variety of festivals and featuring a range of languages;
- note and message pads;
- ready-made booklets of different sizes;
- a typewriter;
- in- and out-trays;
- felt-tip pens, biros, pencils, pens, crayons, a stapler, a hole-punch, rubber stamps, glue, labels, pencil sharpener, Sellotape, string, paper clips, ring binders, scissors, rulers;
- old diaries and calendars;
- line guides and borders;
- a paper trimmer;
- Letraset, stencils;
- a waste bin;
- reference materials such as alphabet books, dictionaries, thesauruses and word banks and lists;
- a postbox which can be emptied at the end of each day;
- a word processor (if possible).

It helps to keep the children's interest if the resources are changed regularly. Children also need to be shown how to use the resources such as the paper trimmer and the stapler. They will need to know how to mount their work and make their own books if they are to work independently and use the area purposefully. The children can also be involved in organizing the writing area. They can make labels for the equipment and write notices for the area. The use of the writing area should be discussed with the class and some of the writing that is produced there can be shared, displayed and responded to by others.

The writing area should invite children to use it. Teachers may write notices such as 'Come and Make a Book' or 'Make a List of your Favourite Books', that encourage children to use it both at set writing times and when they can make choices about their activities. Written suggestions about what children might write when they choose to use the area, such as an invitation to rewrite a story that has recently been shared with the class or to write to a child who is away from school, can maintain the children's involvement in using the writing area. The writing area should be a quiet place where writing is seen as an enjoyable and purposeful activity. If it is available for use at any time by the children it can give them the chance to experiment with writing for their own purposes and at their own pace, without pressure for particular results and usually without needing much adult intervention. Used in this way it can help to foster independence since it can be a place where children are in control of the writing process. It can give children the space to initiate and carry out ideas of their own.

The writing area can also be used to display writing, including writing in a variety of scripts and languages, writing from home, a range of handwriting styles, writing that has been received by the class and writing that has been done at school. Writing that is displayed may reflect current events in the classroom or for the children. The writing area can demonstrate writing used for a variety of purposes and in a variety of styles.

The relationship between reading and writing

An important part of the writing environment in the classroom is provided by books. This includes books that are in the library or book corner, books that are taken home by the children, books that are read to children, books that are made by children, books that are made by the teacher, and big books that are shared with the class.

Learning to read and learning to write can be seen as mutually supportive activities. Reading involves re-creating an author's meaning: it demands that the reader understands what has been written. Writing is the production of meaning in a written form with the expectation that the meaning can be understood and retrieved later by oneself or by others. Both reading and writing are concerned with understanding and using written symbols. Looking at books and experimenting with writing involve important literacy lessons that inform children about how writing works, what it can do and how they can use it.

Learning to read supports learning to write in many ways. From books children learn that print carries a message and as they begin to write they will want their writing to convey meaning. When reading they learn that symbols used in writing are not arbitrary: writers use a set of symbols with a particular form. They can see that writing is arranged in a particular way. In the English language it moves from left to right and top to bottom on a page. Spaces separate words and punctuation is used to separate ideas. As children read they are engaging in a visual examination of words and as they read aloud they are using the graphophonic aspects of written language; both of these are important in helping to increase children's awareness of letter shapes and in developing their knowledge about spelling. Experience with reading introduces children to the way written language is used in terms of pattern, style and explicitness. Written language is used in particular ways that have to be experienced and understood before they can be produced. Children may also learn about structuring their own writing by thinking about how different sorts of texts are organized. When stories are shared with children, teachers are familiarizing children with the notion of authorship. As children realize that books are written by people, they can be introduced to the idea that they too can be authors and produce texts for others to read. Books and other forms of text provide ideas for writing – in the words of Smith (1982), 'composition is stimulated by reading'. From their experiences with text, children may learn about the uses, structure and style of many different types of writing. For reading to benefit writing development as much as possible, it is essential that children have access to a wide range of good-quality books which present a range of ideas, styles and organizational structures.

Writing supports reading by reinforcing the visual aspects of language and the meaningful aspects of print. It helps children to become conscious of the relationship between the sounds of words and the way that they are written down. It can lead to the production of the children's own reading material. Shared writing encourages children to pool their knowledge of the writing system, of what words look like and of how they are spelt. Maybe because children are being encouraged to think about the sound and sight of words as they write, 'It has been found that children who are used to writing independently demonstrate greater phonological awareness than children who are used to copying under teachers' writing' (Barrs and Thomas, 1991). If, in addition, time with groups and individuals is given to looking at words and spelling patterns, 'their growing knowledge of how words are constructed will support their reading' (Barrs and Thomas, 1991). Thus it is important that children have a great many opportunities to share, read and discuss books with others, both at school and at home.

Writing and role play

The classroom environment can not always provide the opportunities for the full range of writing that children encounter in the world outside school. Role play is one way of extending the range of purposes, audiences and variety of writing available to children in the classroom. It is also a means of demonstrating the variety and purpose of writing. As the Programme of Study for writing, spelling and handwriting at key stage 1 (DES, 1990) states, 'Pupils should write in a wide range of activities. Early "play" writing, e.g. in a play house, class shop, office, hospital should be encouraged and respected.' The non-statutory guidance for writing (NCC, 1990) expands on this and offers the following advice: 'At KS1 children develop a sense of the variety of written language if writing is a purposeful activity (e.g. when a role-play area is used for a travel agency or a post office).'

It is customary to set up a role-play area in the classroom that arises from the theme that is being undertaken by the class. For example, a clinic or a hospital might be set up to link with work on growth. Alternatively a visit can lead to the creation of a role-play area. A visit to a fire station could lead to a fire station control room being set up in the classroom.

Whatever the type of role-play area, it is important that children have some knowledge and experience of the context to support them as they engage in the writing activities that may arise. When setting up the area it might be appropriate to ask the children to write such things as the signs, notices, menus and price lists that will become part of the play area. The children may also benefit from the teacher joining in and modelling the types of writing that are appropriate, for example writing a shopping list or taking a phone message. It is important to make sure that all the children understand how the activity is set up, what is expected of them and what is the purpose of the writing that emerges.

The sort of writing that might emerge from setting up a hospital in the classroom could include:

- patient notes;
- appointment books;
- prescriptions;
- forms;
- patient charts;
- telephone messages;
- get-well cards;
- letters to and from patients.

If the play area is used as a home corner this too can be a valuable source of literacy activities. Children can write books to read to the dolls, invitations for a dolls' party, greeting cards, telephone messages, shopping lists, notes for the milk deliverer, items in a diary, labels for jars and containers, and forms such as football coupons. It is useful to use the home corner to illustrate the different sorts of writing that may be found in the home. To this end it might contain magazines, newspapers, letters, greeting cards, postcards, recipe books, a calendar, a telephone directory, the *TV Times* or *Radio Times*, packets and containers with writing on them such as washing powder and cereal cartons. It should also have resources for writing such as pens, paper, postcards and notepads which are present in most homes.

By using writing in role-play activities, children may come to recognize the uses of writing and the many types of writing that exist. They will have been given the opportunity to experiment with writing in a relaxed environment. The writing that is produced by the children need not be assessed, improved or redrafted but, by observing children writing in play situations, the teacher can gain insights into their understanding of the writing process and seek to extend this in the more formal writing sessions that take place in the classroom.

Writing across the curriculum

Writing is both part of a distinct curriculum area, English, and a part of every other area of the curriculum. It is easy to identify writing as a part of the English curriculum when children are writing stories, poems or letters. However, the starting point for writing may well be science, technology, geography or history. The children may write up a recipe as part of their investigation of change in science. They may describe and evaluate how they made a musical instrument as part of a technology session so that others can copy their idea. The focus may be on geography if children are planning a route from the school to a local park in preparation for a class picnic. Writing can arise from history if the children are compiling a set of questions to ask a visitor to the school about his childhood in the 1950s. Because writing can arise from every part of the curriculum, the teacher can provide a variety of writing activities that can be written in a variety of forms.

There should also be opportunities for children to write personally at school. Children may have their own private journals where they are free to write anything they like without it being read by others. When children write in journals they may be organizing their thoughts, recording feelings or experimenting with different forms of writing. The opportunities for writing and the possible types of writing that can emerge in school are plentiful and varied. Writing does not need to be a distinct part of the curriculum only taking place with status during 'creative writing lessons'.

Writing activities to support developmental writing

The writing activities that form the writing curriculum for the class or the school should as far as possible have an audience and a purpose that extends beyond the teacher and her requirement that the children should write. They should be meaningful and motivating for all the children. Activities that fulfil these criteria include:

- labels, captions and commentaries for paintings, models and displays;
- information and story-books written by the children for others to read;
- collections of poems written by the children;
- cards;
- letters that receive a response from others or written to thank visitors to the school;
- invitations to parents and carers to attend events at school;
- records of books read or projects that have been undertaken;
- instructions to users of games or equipment;
- reviews of books and posters to display in the book corner;
- charts or graphs recording surveys and discoveries;
- newspapers for the class or school;
- information leaflets about the school for new entrants to the class or school.

Not all writing at school will have an outside audience. Some writing will take the form of drafts, notes, plans and personal writing. Writing in this form may be used to organize thinking and ideas.

Some writing is done as a basis for thought. The form of the writing will be determined by the needs of the child and will vary from the whole text to points forming and aide-memoire. Writing used to organise thinking is perhaps one of the most personal forms and is frequently left incomplete and rarely published.

(NCC, 1989, p. C 16, para 12.7)

When setting writing tasks it may be useful to ask oneself the following questions:

- Who is to read the writing?
- What is this writing for?
- What will happen to the writing when it is finished?
- How might this affect the way children set about it?
- Is it appropriate to draft, redraft, put it on tape, use the word processor, work with others, publish or display it?
- How might it be presented – as connected prose, a list, a diagram or a commentary?

A carefully planned writing curriculum where time is given for children to produce purposeful and careful pieces of writing motivates children as writers and extends their repertoire of writing skills and styles.

Shared writing
Shared writing refers to the times when a group of children compose a

text together with the teacher acting as the scribe for the group. When children are more familiar with the format they may take over some of the scribing but initially it is more helpful if the teacher does this. It is generally best organized by having the children sitting as a group on the carpet and the teacher writing on large sheets of paper on a flip chart or an easel. It is essential that all the children can see the writing.

The activity usually begins by the teacher and children discussing the topic that will be written about. If the activity is new to the class it may be best to use shared writing to retell a familiar story, write a letter, produce an account of a visit, make a sign to go with a display in the classroom or to compose a poem, as these have a clear structure that can be followed by the children. It is important to be clear about the aims and purposes of the writing with the children as this will affect the style and content of the writing. After the initial discussion the teacher takes the pupils through all the processes of writing as she scribes for the pupils. The first stage is to brainstorm ideas to be included in the writing. As the children contribute their ideas the teacher records these as a list or in a spider diagram. After collecting the ideas on content the group consider which ideas should come at the beginning, middle and end of the writing. The teacher then numbers the ideas in the order that they will occur in the text to form a plan. Whilst retaining the plan for reference, the children and the teacher begin to compose the writing. The initial ideas are reworked, words are changed and sentences are composed as the group focus on the writing. At the end of this stage the first draft of the writing, probably containing false starts and crossing out, is complete. The first draft is read through and may be revised or edited before the final draft is produced by the teacher or the pupils.

A piece of shared writing may take a number of sessions to complete. This provides a useful message about the permanence of text and how it helps people to remember ideas. It also signals that writing that is worth doing need not be completed in one session. Reading and reviewing what has been written at the beginning of each session may lead to further revisions and may help pupils to see the benefits of rereading a piece of writing. Writing may benefit from taking place over a longer period than one session since the writer has had time to think about what has been written and may bring new ideas to the writing.

The completed writing may be copied out by the children to form individual letters or books that they can illustrate. With a long piece individual children may copy out one section of the text that consists of the writing for one page of a class book. They can then illustrate their page. Alternatively the teacher may make the final draft of the writing and the children may illustrate the writing for a large book that can be used in class during shared-reading sessions. Sometimes the teacher may stop scribing before the final draft of the writing and the children can use the plan and the draft to compose their own individual ending to the story, poem, letter or account. Whatever the final outcome of shared-writing sessions it is important that the teacher has thought beforehand about how the activity will end.

Shared writing encourages children to reflect on all aspects of the writing process. The children see all the stages of reflecting, planning, drafting, editing, evaluating and redrafting taking place and from this model they can learn valuable lessons about how they might work on their own writing in class. As the children see the teacher writing, their attention may be drawn to spelling patterns, punctuation, word boundaries and layout of text as well as the patterns and conventions associated with different genres of written language. The way that writing works is made explicit during the discussion and the modelling.

Writing in this way enables children to work collaboratively and to draw on each other's strengths and knowledge. As the transcriptional aspects of writing are taken over by the teacher the children can focus on the composition and, as a result, can often produce longer, more complex texts than they could do alone. In particular, less confident or less able writers benefit from shared writing since they can see that writing does not have to be perfect at the first attempt and that writing is as much about composition as transcription. Such children may experience a great sense of satisfaction from seeing their ideas in print.

The skills and practices that are modelled during shared-writing sessions provide a structure that the children might use when they write and the teacher can expect these routines to be adopted by older first-school children in their individual or paired writing. Depending on age, experience and level of confidence, groups of children may be able to work on shared writing alone or with very little teacher help. Younger children benefit from seeing how the transcription of writing takes place and this will help them in their writing.

Scribing

More experienced writers such as older children, parents, carers or other adult volunteers, can be invited into the classroom to write with and for the children. They can transcribe for individuals or small groups of children, leaving the children free to concentrate on the composition of text. While they write they can discuss the choice of words, spelling, the use of punctuation and layout with the writers. They can also act as prompts if the composition dries up and they can encourage the children to read and reread what has been written and to reflect on the text. More experienced writers may do all the writing involved in planning and writing first drafts. They can write by hand or on the computer. They may tape-record a child's story and then work with the child as she writes her story using the tape recording as a first draft. Before volunteers start to work with the pupils it is essential that they know exactly what is required of them. The teacher needs to spend some time explaining the way she works and the way that she would like them to work with the children. The Programme of Study for writing, spelling and handwriting, key stage 1, states that the use of experienced writers can enable children 'to compose at greater length than they can manage to write down by themselves' (DES, 1990 p. B7). The non-statutory guidance expands on the benefits of adults writing for and with children when it suggests that children 'can also see how writing should be tackled (by watching adults writing, by having help from adults as scribes, and writing alongside them)'. The satisfaction children gain from seeing their words in print is enormous and may motivate children to want to write alone.

The writing conference

A conference is a time for a child to discuss her writing with the teacher. It can last for anything from two minutes to as long as the child needs and classroom organization permits. The main aim is for the teacher to find out what difficulties the child thinks she has with writing and to provide ways forward for her. The conference may begin with the child reading or summarizing her writing so far. The teacher then asks the child questions about the writing. These questions might include:

- How is your writing going?
- What do you think you will do next?
- Could you add anything else that will interest the reader?
- How might you insert more information about your topic in what you have written so far?
- What do you do when you aren't sure about how to spell a word?
- How do you work out where to put full stops in your writing?
- What will you do with your writing when it is finished?

The questions are intended to focus the child's attention on her writing and to find out what writing strategies she uses. Depending on the child, the teacher might provide help with the composition or the transcription of a piece of writing. The conference should occur as the child is engaged on her first and subsequent drafts so that she can revise and improve her writing as a result of the conference. In the Programme of Study for writing for key stage 1 (DES, 1990) it is suggested that 'Pupils should discuss their writing frequently, talking about the varied types and purposes of writing, e.g. list, poem, story, recipe. Teachers should talk about correct spelling and its patterns, about punctuation, and should introduce pupils to such terms as punctuation, letter, capital letter, full stop, question mark.'

Holding a conference is like listening to a child read. In it the teacher is trying to listen to the child write and to respond to the strengths and weaknesses that the child reveals as she talks about the process of writing for her. The teacher responds to what the child can do as well as what the child finds difficult. Graves (1983) describes through detailed case histories how conferencing can add to the teaching and learning of writing and how it can lead to 'dramatic changes in children's writing', since it is an opportunity for the teacher to provide the help that the child identifies as important and that meets her needs in that particular piece of writing.

During the conference the teacher should be aware of the context, purpose and audience for the writing. She needs to be aware of the child's attitude to writing and to temper her comments to fit the child's effort and feelings about herself as a writer. When she receives the writing she needs to understand the message, analyse the composition, analyse the transcription and in consultation with the child decide on what the child should do next.

Response partners

The idea of pairing children to act as consultants for each other's writing developed during the course of the National Writing Project and was reported in the resulting publications (National Writing Project, 1989a, 1989b), notably *Responding to and Assessing Writing* in which a case-study of two reception-age children working in this way is documented. In their pairs children listen to or read their partner's writing and comment on how the writing might be improved or extended. They can comment on clarity of meaning and order as well as helping with spelling and punctuation. Children need to be instructed about how they can best help to improve the work of others and they will probably benefit from their own experiences of working in this way during conferences and shared-writing sessions with the teacher.

Drafting and redrafting

Few writers have the skill of producing perfect writing at the first attempt. Most writers need to draft important pieces of writing before producing a final copy. Children too need to be introduced to this method of working. In the Programme of Study for writing for key stage 1 (DES, 1990, p. 36) it is stated that

Pupils working towards level 3 should be taught to recognise that writing involves:

— decision making – when the context (the specific situation, precise purpose and intended audience) is established;
— planning – when initial thoughts and the framework are recorded and ordered;
— drafting – when initial thoughts are developed, evaluated and reshaped by expansion, addition or amendment to the text.

The process of drafting encourages children to shape and reshape their ideas on paper, on the computer or on tape before producing the final version of their writing. It encourages children to reflect on their writing and to evaluate and self-correct as they read through what they have written. If children are to spend this amount of time on a piece of writing then it is essential that the writing task is important enough to demand this degree of attention from the child. It is also important that before the child writes she knows the purpose and audience for her writing as this will affect the content, style and organization of the writing. For example, a letter to a friend reads very differently, is set out in a different way and includes different sorts of information to a letter written to a stranger. Not all writing needs to be drafted; it depends on its purpose and audience.

During shared-writing sessions the teacher models for the children the ways in which writers draft and redraft their writing. She may need to give children further explanations and examples of how to draft and redraft, and why it is helpful to work in this way, before children are confident with the procedure. Before writing the first draft of a piece of writing the first stage for the writer is to focus on what she is about to write. She may spend time recollecting and remembering information, incidents or feelings. She then needs to make a note of the ideas that she had thought of, maybe in the form of a spider diagram or a list. This brainstorm may contain key words and expressions as well as ideas. This period of recollection and planning may be helped by drawing either one picture or a sequence of pictures that help the writer to organize her thoughts and reflect on what she is going to write. Next the ideas need to be organized into a coherent plan, maybe by making a list or numbering the ideas in sequence.

After the first stage of thinking about the ideas and making a preliminary outline the writer is ready to write. The first draft of the writing is about getting it down fast, without worrying about the transcription elements such as spelling, punctuation or handwriting. As long as the child can read her own writing there is no need to interrupt the creative flow of the writing. At this stage the child may make false starts and rethink as she writes and this may result in what looks like a messy piece of work with misspellings and crossing out. This does not represent careless or poor work. This is what an adult writer's first draft often looks like and represents the writer's struggle with the process of translating thoughts and ideas clearly into the written form. There is no need for the child to use an eraser to conceal mistakes at this stage; an adult writer would be unlikely to use a rubber on a first draft, crossing out is far quicker and interrupts one's thoughts far less. It is also unnecessary for the child to check her spellings by asking the teacher or consulting a dictionary. As long as the spellings can be read back these can be checked after the first draft has been written. The mistakes that a child makes at this stage provide a useful insight for the teacher into the difficulties that a child may have in writing and how the child tackles writing since they may indicate thinking in progress. They may also provide starting points for discussion during a writing conference.

When the first draft is complete it is time for the child to read through her writing. She can look for clarity of meaning and change words, phrases and sentences to make a more satisfactory piece of writing. She can also proofread for spelling and punctuation errors. It is at this stage that the child might use a dictionary to check or find spellings. Problems that the child can not resolve herself, such as parts of the writing that do not make sense or spellings that she thinks may be wrong, can be indicated by the child using a highlighter pen or underlining words with a different-coloured pen. After rereading her work carefully the child may be ready for a writing conference with the teacher. The child and the teacher can discuss the work so far and see if further revision or more ideas are necessary. It is also at this stage that the teacher might teach the child some spellings and demonstrate correct letter formation. If the child has a response partner she may read the writing through and suggest ideas for improvement as well.

The writing may go through another draft to incorporate all the suggestions for improvement that the child has received and to include new ideas or sections that the child feels would improve the piece. Alternatively, after the first draft the child may move straight on to the final draft. At this stage the child should be clear about how she is going to present the work. Is it going to be in the form of a book, a letter or for a wall display? This may determine layout and choice of writing materials. The focus at this stage is on presentation. The child needs to write carefully with clear handwriting and attention to spelling if the work is to be read by others. The teacher can expect the child's work to reflect the help that she has received from others. The child will at this stage begin to incorporate illustrations into her writing and will at the end of the final draft have a piece of writing that is satisfying for the writer and interesting for others to read.

The time spent on drafting and redrafting will vary depending on the child's age and experience as a writer. Very young children may plan through pictures, talk to the teacher about what they are going to write and produce a sentence of their own that is read to the teacher. The teacher may then discuss the writing with the child and either write the correct version under the child's writing or correct one or two errors and ask the child to rewrite the sentences incorporating the corrections in the final draft.

Older, more experienced writers who can write at greater length can be expected to go through all the stages of planning, editing and producing a final draft. It is very difficult to assign ages to these procedures but very young children may be nursery, reception and Year 1 pupils, and older children may include Year 1, Year 2 and Year 3 pupils.

In order for drafting to work, the class has to be organized so that a piece of writing can be worked on over a period of days. One day's work in writing may only cover the planning and first-draft stage. Children need to be able to store their first drafts in their own writing folder or in their first-draft book. They can then return to their writing the next day.

Drafting takes pupils through the real stages of writing. It enables pupils to take risks since it does not matter if they make mistakes in a draft as these can be rectified and improved later. It helps pupils to focus on composition and content rather than transcription and can result in a very satisfying piece of writing of which they can be proud.

Publishing

Publishing means making the child's writing public, mainly through books but also in other forms such as posters, notices or letters. Not every piece of writing done by a child needs to be published. The child and the teacher should discuss whether a piece of writing should be published. The original purpose of the writing as well as the quality of the finished product may influence the decision. Personal writing, diaries, notes, diagrams or plans may never have been intended for an audience beyond the writer or the teacher. Publishing should be viewed as the end of a long process where the teacher works through the drafts with the child and both agree that the writing is good enough to be published. Quality must take account of each child's experience and the degree of effort that has been invested in the writing. This will differ from child to child even in the same class or age group.

The subject matter and the presentation may determine what form the publication takes. Accounts of learning and discovery may become part of a display. Captions, labels and explanations may be placed next to models or drawings. Stories or information may be published in books that are placed in the class library to be read by the writer and other children in the class.

Making Books

Making books and writing stories that are read by the author and others is highly motivating for children. It enables them to feel that their writing is valued and provides a purpose and an incentive for writing. Through making books children's writing can reach a wider audience than the class teacher. Books can be read in assemblies and put in the school or class library. They can be added to the class stock and if appropriate can be photocopied and produced in multiple copies for use as group readers. Book making is one way of providing texts that are relevant to the particular community within a school. Books can be written that reflect the locality and feature the children in the class as central characters, and they can be produced as dual texts with heritage languages appropriate to the school written to accompany an English text.

In the process of book making, children can find out how books work. They can investigate how different kinds of books are organized. Some books have an index, a list of contents, are organized into chapters, contain notes about the author, have summaries, include dedications and feature reviews by others. The children may reproduce these features in the books they write. In addition, when writing the book the children will have to plan, draft, revise and produce a best copy either on the word processor or by hand so they will be going through all the stages of writing as they aim to write publishable material.

When teachers suggest that children make a book for publication, they need to be clear about the implicit messages they may be giving children about authorship. Consideration will need to be given to providing opportunities for the child to:
— identify the audience for the book;
— understand the needs of the audience;
— compose the text;
— make decisions about the organisation of the text;
— share the writing with peers to gain another viewpoint;
— have opportunities to re-shape the writing;
— have a choice of published format. (NCC, 1989, p. C15, para 11.8)

The repertoire of content and format for books at school is vast but it can include:

- poetry;
- imaginative stories;
- personal stories;
- information books;
- biographies;
- recipes;

- jokes;
- cartoons;
- stories based around superheroes;
- rewrites of well-known stories;
- dual-text stories;
- stories in home languages;
- books containing records of work undertaken during a theme;
- books written for younger children;
- books made by parents and children;
- cumulative books such as reviews of favourite books;
- flap or pop-up books;
- zig-zag or concertina books;
- big books;
- little books;
- instant books.

In addition there might be

> — notes, observation books and diaries produced independently and informally in the imaginative play area or as a result of practical activities;
> — stories written collaboratively, with a small group, an older child writing with/for a younger child, with the teacher as 'scribe', with other adults.

> Books made in class may be informal stapled 'mini-books' or photographic sequenced books, books with acetate inserts for reader response, adventure game books, comic books, books with audio tapes, group magazines and instruction booklets.
>
> (NCC, 1989, p. C15, para 11.7)

In order to produce books, children will need access to a variety of materials, probably all those available in the writing area. Sometimes books can be ready-made but it is valuable for the children to make their own books and decide on their own choice of design and format. This can be a useful technology and mathematics exercise for pupils. Teachers might like to display instructions about ways of making books in the writing area. Useful and stimulating sources of book-making techniques for teachers and children can be found in *Making Books* (Chapman and Robson, 1991) and *Developing Literacy through Making Books* (Johnson, 1990).

Conclusion

Writing at school should represent our understanding of how children learn to write and include activities and resources that reflect this understanding. The curriculum should take account of what children know, of writing as a communicative act, of audience and purpose, of variety and of activities that enable children to write in a meaningful way. The classroom should provide a context within which children's writing can develop and within which the teacher and the children work together to enhance achievement. This chapter has presented practitioners with a number of suggestions about the ways in which they can organize the physical resources of the classroom and the activities that form part of the writing curriculum.

Questions about writing in practice

Q. Why should I change my writing practice to that of developmental writing?
A. The answer to this question could be extremely long. However, the short answer is that there are many benefits to both children and children's written work. These benefits to the children include improved attitude towards writing, enjoyment of writing and enhanced self-esteem. Improvements in the writing that is produced include better quality, more detail and longer, more thoughtful pieces of writing. A teacher who has recently changed her practice said, 'the children write more and in more detail . . . it really works'. In brief, this approach builds on and extends what children already know about writing and represents one aspect of developmental learning.

Q. When is it best to introduce developmental writing?
A. When a child first starts school is the obvious answer. However, it can be successfully introduced later, particularly if it follows the agreement of a whole-school policy on developmental writing. Children very quickly adjust to routines and expectations at school. 'Having a go' and working without erasers will not take long to introduce if children are given reasons for these practices and if they are applied consistently.

Q. How should children be organized for writing activities?
A. Normally children should be arranged within mixed-ability groups. Children often learn from each other as well as from the teacher or adult. Children can also work in collaborative pairs and in adult-led groups for shared writing.

Q. Should writing always take place in the morning when children are at their freshest?
A. Children are usually at their best when they are interested in what they are doing, whatever this is. If they are interested in their writing they will concentrate in the afternoon as well as they concentrate during

morning sessions. It is easier for the teacher to work with groups of children rather than the whole class on writing and for this reason it is usual to plan for different groups to write throughout the day. Sometimes some children who are working on a long project may spend a whole day writing. If this happens they would then work at other activities the next day and might do less writing than usual for the next few days.

Q.   Do drafting and redrafting have a place in developmental writing?
A.   Yes. If a piece of work is to be made public in a book or on a display, the teacher and child may work on one or two points from, for example, presentation, spelling, organization or ideas before the writing is copied out again in its final version. To make redrafting worth while the piece of work must have a reason for being written and an audience beyond the teacher or child. As the child progresses at writing it is important that she is shown how adult writers write, that is by planning, drafting and redrafting until they are satisfied with what has been written.

4

Spelling

Introduction

This chapter is divided into three sections. In the first section, 'The nature of spelling' common difficulties that writers encounter when spelling and the various strategies that adults draw upon when spelling unfamiliar words are examined. The second section 'How spelling develops', presents a developmental model of learning about spelling which indicates that inexperienced spellers are often able to draw upon phonic strategies when spelling, but that this is not sufficient to enable them to spell accurately. As spelling is a visual skill, phonic strategies can be unreliable and are only one of a range of strategies that can be used and are used by competent spellers. The final section, 'Supporting children's development in spelling', presents a number of practical ideas that teachers may use when teaching children to spell. These are intended to extend children's strategies by concentrating on developing visual and memory skills for spelling.

The nature of spelling

Learning to spell in the English language can be as complicated as learning to understand a pilot's flight-deck. Very few adults spell every word they need or use confidently, accurately and without hesitation. Look at the list of words below and try to test your spelling by identifying the words that are spelt correctly. As you do this exercise try to identify the strategies you use to make your decision.

    accidentally
    assassin
    ecstasy
    embarrass
    gauge

liaison
moccasin
parralell
queue
siege

The answers to this spelling test are given at the end of this chapter.

However you fared at this test it is unlikely that you only used one strategy to help you decide which words were correct or incorrect. Sounding or saying each syllable of each word slowly would probably not provide the information needed to decide how many s's or c's are contained in the word *moccasin*. As you looked at the list you may have asked yourself, 'Does this look right?' and 'What do I know about the English language that will help me to decide how these words should be written?'

Adults frequently call upon a variety of strategies to help them spell correctly. These range from using aids such as dictionaries and spelling checkers to personal strategies such as sounding out or pronouncing in an exaggerated form a word that they are unsure of. Slowly pronouncing each syllable of a word such as *desperate* might still leave doubt as to whether the correct spelling is *desperate* or *desparate*. To check this a writer might write down both versions, look carefully at each and ask the question, 'Does this look right?', and if still unsure write down another version of the same word to compare the arrangement of letters before selecting a spelling of the word that seems to be correct. Sometimes writers might use a known spelling to provide clues about the spelling of a more difficult word, for example using *finite* to spell *definite*, or *lie* to spell *believe*. It is also possible that we use our knowledge of how the English language is constructed to clarify our ideas about how to spell certain words, for example prefixes and suffixes do not affect the spelling of the root of a word, they are merely added on. This knowledge may help when spelling a word such as *disappointment*: one may know how to spell *appointment* and can then add the prefix *dis* without having to agonize about how many s's are found in it. Once clear about the root of a word such as *appoint* it is not difficult to spell other words in this family such as *disappointing* and *disappointed*. Adults also draw upon knowledge of likely letter combinations that are to be found in English when spelling: it is rare to have problems with letter strings such as *ing* or *tion*. Just as adults use a variety of strategies to aid their spelling, children too need to tackle spelling in a number of ways.

Learning to spell is an important part of learning to write. Correct spelling makes writing more readable and enables the writer to communicate more easily with her audience. However, it is not the main focus of writing. The separate attainment targets for writing, spelling and hand-writing remind us that spelling is only part of the writing curriculum. It is easy when reading children's writing to focus on spelling errors first and the content of what was written second, perhaps because spelling provides something more tangible to comment on than style, structure or choice of vocabulary. This is perhaps even more the case in the very early stages of writing when children's writing can be very simple and brief. Unfortunately, if teachers do this, particularly with children who are just beginning to write, they risk inhibiting children's desire to write. Too much emphasis on correct spelling may produce writers who are frightened to 'have a go' alone and who play safe with the words they use in their writing, choosing to use words that they think they can spell correctly rather than more adventurous words that add colour and atmosphere. How often does one see the word *nice* used in writing at school rather than words such as *wonderful, interesting* or *exciting*? If the role of spelling in writing is overemphasized, teachers may be teaching children that learning to write is just about learning to spell and that if you can not spell you can not write. It is possible to transmit this message in many ways, not just by over-stringent correction of children's spelling errors but also by only displaying perfectly spelt work, by training children in the indiscriminate use of word books and by encouraging children to use erasers to correct every mistake they make as they are putting their thoughts on to paper. It is important to maintain a realistic awareness of what children may be expected to achieve in unaided spelling as they begin to discover how the spelling system of the English language works and to let this sense of proportion guide the teaching of spelling and the assessment and correction of writing by young writers.

How spelling develops

Research suggests that the acquisition of spelling skills can be viewed as a developmental process (Read, 1986; Temple *et al.* 1988). Researchers have identified stages in learning to spell that writers seem to pass through as they attempt to work out some systematic regularities and patterns that might underlie spelling.

The first stage has been called the pre-phonemic or pre-literate stage of spelling development. At this stage children are attempting to imitate the writing that they have seen in the world around them. They are making their first attempts to join in with the communicative act of writing and in doing so are making their first discoveries about writing. The writing that is produced may take the form of scribbles or pretend writing and may incorporate odd numerals or letters that are found in the child's name. The writing may look like writing but because there is no application of any sound–symbol knowledge the text is unreadable although the child may be able to explain what she intended to write. Figure 4.1 is an example of the pre-phonemic stage.

Figure 4.1

During the next stage, known as the early or semi-phonemic stage, the child shows an awareness of the alphabetic and phonic principles of the English language. The child begins to use letter names to represent words, for example R for *are* and NIT for *night*. Spelling such as this indicates that the child appreciates the sound–symbol nature of the language and is able to exploit her understanding of this complex relationship. Elements of this stage may persist for some time and are helpful to the speller and the reader in communicating and understanding the message. In Figure 4.2, John, who is at this stage, has written *tiyl laya* for *tile layer*.

Figure 4.2

In the third stage, known as the phonetic, the child recognizes that sounds in words can be represented by letters, more letters are included in the words and the child's words become more complete. Examples of words using this phonic knowledge include *baf* for *bath*, *smtis* for *Smarties*, and *cis* for *kiss*. In the list of words in Figure 4.3, *telvishn* and *clok* are examples of the spelling of a child at the phonetic stage.

As the child moves towards the final correct stage of spelling she moves away from being almost wholly dependent on phonic strategies and into what is known as the transitional stage. Increased experiences of reading and awareness of correct models of writing give children an awareness of the visual aspects of words. Children are still aware of how words sound but they combine this with a knowledge of how words look. Increasingly they begin to write words that look right,

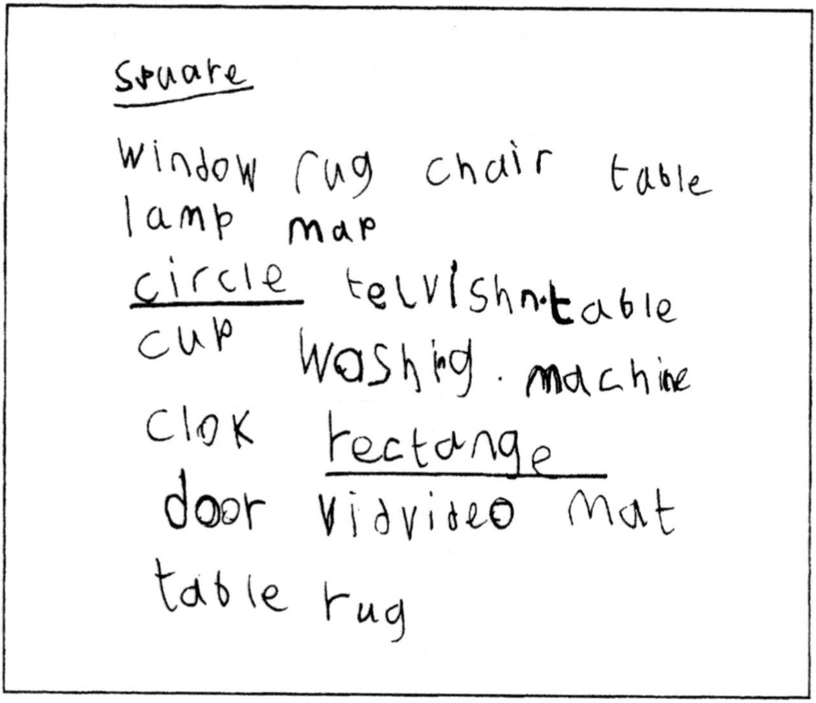

Figure 4.3

showing an understanding of letter combinations that are frequently found in the English language. This can result in spellings such as *howld* for *hold* and *coloer* for *colour*. In Figure 4.4, *know* instead of *no* is a good example of this.

The final stage is when correct spellings are produced almost all the time. At this level children are seen to be using a combination of strategies, including letter sounds, letter names, letter strings and visual strategies, to produce clear approximations or correct spellings of short and multi-syllabic words. The book review written by Paul, aged 7 (Figure 4.5), is a good example of this.

Supporting children's development in spelling

An appreciation of how children learn to spell and the spelling strategies used by adults is important since it enables teachers to identify good errors and establish a framework for teaching spelling. The non-statutory guidance (NCC, 1990) suggests that 'Teachers should help children to develop from invented spelling towards conventional

Figure 4.4

accuracy. The invented spellings of the young child need to be interpreted because they show the use of logical rules. Teachers need to assess the child's level of understanding of the spelling system and provide help.'

The first step in assisting children with spelling is to assess what they can do and then to consider how they can be helped to improve. Researchers suggest that until children reach the transitional stage of spelling development they are unlikely to benefit from instruction about spelling. Children need to have some understanding of the principles of English orthography and the opportunity to produce their own invented spelling before they can understand and absorb instruction about

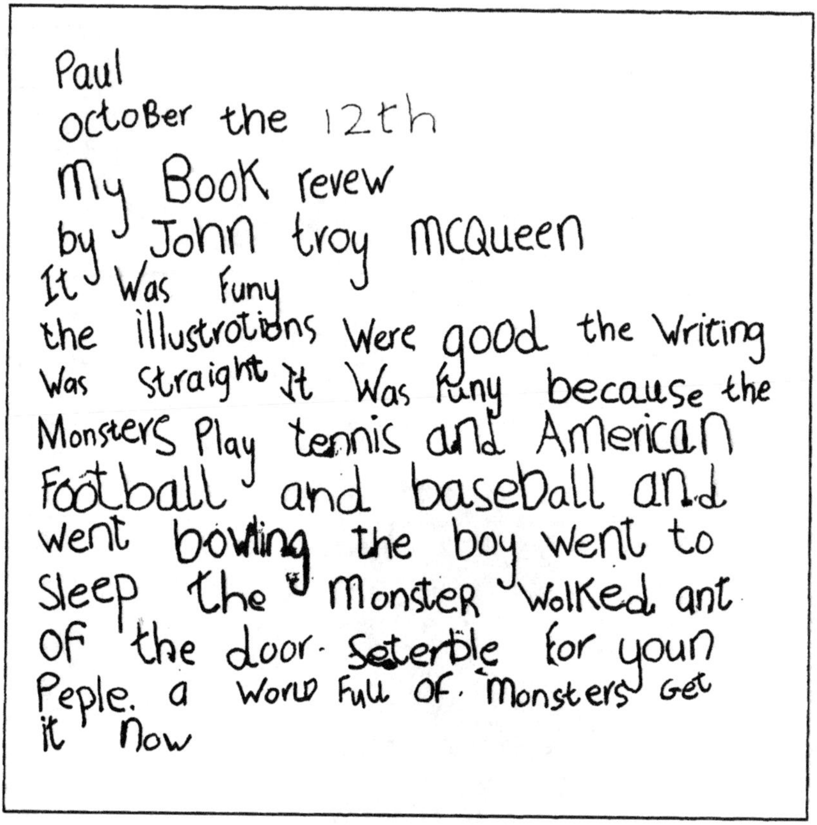

Paul
octoBer the 12th
My BooK revew
by John troy McQueen
It Was funy
the illustrotions Were good the Writing
Was straight It Was funy because the
Monsters Play tennis and American
Football and baseball and
went bowling the boy went to
Sleep the monsteR wolked ant
of the door. Saterble for youn
Peple. a Word Full of Monsters Get
it now

Figure 4.5

correct spelling (Whitehead, 1990; Palmer, 1991). Indeed it has been
suggested that too early an emphasis on correctness can make children
anxious about writing and, inhibit the experiments with writing, and
thus the experiments with words, that would give them an early understanding of principles of spelling. None the less, whatever the age of the
child and the stage she has reached it is likely that she will benefit from
seeing correct models of print since the experience of looking at words
and the accumulation of experience give her insights into how English is
written. Such models of print may occur in classroom displays, in books
that are read to and by children and in the writing that the teacher does in
front of the child.

There is considerable evidence to suggest that accurate spellers draw
on visual rather than phonic strategies when spelling (Peters, 1985).
Auditory strategies are notoriously unreliable aids to spelling as the

earlier example of *cis* for *kiss* demonstrates. English is not a truly alphabetic or phonically regular language and to treat it as such causes as many
problems as it resolves. If, for example, we try to spell a word such as
through simply by sounding it out we can get into a terrific muddle. In the
first place, *through* could be and is represented by the letters *threw*; context rather than sound determines which set of letters is appropriate.
Moreover, *ough* may also be represented by *ou* as in *you*, *u* as in *pru-
dent*, *oo* as in *boo*, *oe* as in *shoe* and *ue* as in *clue*, and there are almost
certainly other ways of representing this sound in English given the
vagaries of the language. In addition, *ough* can also stand for the *off*
sound as in *cough*, the *ow* sound in *bough* and the *up* sound in *hiccough*!

The developmental model indicates that inexperienced spellers almost
always draw upon phonic strategies without having to be formally
taught. Children who spell in this way are making good progress in
spelling since readable spellings that communicate meaning, such as
wos, *littel* and *stopt*, may result, but children need to proceed beyond this
stage. To teach and overemphasize the role of auditory or phonic strategies when helping children to spell may prevent children from developing beyond the phonetic stage of spelling development. Rather than
limiting or reinforcing children's own strategies it is important to extend
their repertoire of approaches to spelling.

Spelling is primarily a visual skill. Good spellers can often 'see' correct
spellings inside their heads, they 'know' by 'looking' at words whether
they are spelled correctly. To help children 'see' and 'know' we have to
give them opportunities to look at and visualize words. The words to
work with are words that are relevant to the child and those that occur in
her writing. The strategies that follow are intended to develop children's
visual awareness and memory for words.

Becoming aware of words

The classroom environment should be one that encourages children to be
aware of and interested in print. Classroom displays, labels and notices
that are regularly drawn to the children's attention lead children to be
aware of words and the arrangement of letters. The teacher can use story
and reading periods to draw attention to print, both in books and beyond
them. For example, after reading the 'Big Book' *Mrs Wishy Washy* (Melser
and Cowley, 1980) with the class the teacher could follow this up by
asking the children to think of words they know that contain the letters
sh. These could be recorded by the teacher on a flip chart while she spells
out the letters. After a list has been compiled the teacher could ask
individual pupils to find particular words on the chart. This activity
involves careful visual examination of words.

The teacher and children can make other collections of words, for

example issuing a written invitation to the children with the heading
'How many words do we know that begin with B or b?' written on the
flip chart. The children can be encouraged to find words themselves and
add them to the collection. This activity can continue for several days. The
collection can be examined daily and the words discussed as a class.
These activities fulfil some of the suggestions given in the non-statutory
guidance about spelling, including:

— reading with the teacher and referring to print such as captions
and lists in the classroom;
— grouping words and looking for common letter clusters in books
and magazines;
— making collections of words related to children's interests and
work in different subjects.

(NCC, 1990, p. B8, para 3.2)

Spelling patterns
Teachers can also talk about words to children in order to help them 'see'
words more clearly. For example, one could list the smaller words contained within the word *heart* – *hear, ear, he* and *art*. After a discussion
about all the words and the letters they contain, the children are more
likely to remember how to spell the original word and may have added
more words to their spelling vocabulary. Children may also remember
some of the spelling patterns found in the English language, in this
instance *ear*. This may help them when spelling other words such as
tear, wear or *bear*. An associated activity is to find a long word that is of
interest to children or drawn from the current theme in the classroom, for
example a word such as *electricity*, and ask the children to make as many
words as possible using the letters that are contained in the word. Other
words to discuss include families of words, for example *stay, staying* and
stayed, and words that have prefixes and suffixes. Such activities will help
children to meet the statements of attainment for attainment target 4 –
spelling – where children are expected to

recognise that spelling has patterns, and begin to apply their knowledge of those patterns in their attempts to spell a wider range of
words [level 2];
show a growing awareness of word families and their relationships
[level 3];
spell correctly, in the course of their own writing, words which
display other main patterns in English spelling [level 4].

Look, cover, remember, write, check
When correcting spellings or giving a child a word that has been

requested it is not helpful to spell the word out using individual letter sounds. It is difficult for a child to take in auditory information and translate it into a visual image. As this approach emphasizes the auditory rather than the visual aspects of spelling it does not provide the child with strategies for future spelling (Peters, 1985). Nor is it helpful to articulate syllables slowly. When each syllable is articulated separately, the emphasis and intonation alter our hearing of the word and may emphasize the wrong parts of the word, for example *stable* could become *stay . . . bull*. If words are spelt out for a child it is more helpful to use letter names as these are always constant, unlike sounds which can vary depending on the word. For example, in the word *circus* the first *c* sounds like *s*, the second *c* like *k*. This may be confusing for a young child.

The most helpful way of giving spellings is to write the word down for the child using the 'look, cover, remember, write, check' routine originally devised by Peters and Cripps (1980) and recommended in the non-statutory guidance for spelling (NCC, 1990). First the teacher writes the word for the child and then asks the child to look at the word and to memorize it. The correct version is then removed or covered and the child is then asked to write the word from memory without help. The child's spelling is then checked against the correct version. If the spelling is correct the child can incorporate the word into her writing. If the word is incorrect the teacher and the child compare the two spellings of the word and identify where the problem lies and then the procedure is repeated.

This strategy helps the child to

1 memorize the correct spelling;
2 look at the whole word;
3 get the overall visual pattern of the word.

This activity is suggested in the Programme of Study for writing for key stage 1 where it is stated that to help with learning accurate spellings teachers can teach 'the children to "look, cover, remember, write, check" in memorising new words', (NCC, 1990)

Positive correction
When correcting children's spelling it is best to work with the errors that arise in what the child is writing. These words are of use and interest to the child and for that reason the correct spelling is more likely to be remembered. Some teachers ask the children to identify the words that cause problems or that they think are incorrect. One way of doing this is to ask children to put a mark such as a dot next to those words that they think are incorrectly spelt and which they would like help with. If the

child has made a good attempt at the word the teacher might write the correct version of the word beneath the child's version and draw attention to the number of letters that are correct in the child's word. The teacher might illustrate this by putting a tick above each of the letters in the child's word that correspond with the letters in the standard spelling of the word. The teacher might then ask the child to look at the letters that are incorrect and compare these with the correct letters. After doing this with one or two identified errors the teacher can then ask the child to follow the 'look, cover, remember, write, check' routine. One or two words from a piece of writing might be corrected in this way.

Having a go

If children are totally stuck on a word the teacher can suggest that they write down as many as they can of the letters that they think are in the word and indicate by lines or dashes where the missing letters are. A word attempted in this way might look like *be___s* for *because*. When the teacher reads through the writing with the child she can fill in the spaces and talk about the word with the child. This strategy encourages less confident children to 'have a go' without feeling that they have got something wrong and indicates to the teacher which words might be tackled first when she is helping the child with her spelling.

Drafting and redrafting

If children are in the habit of producing first and second drafts of their writing, help with spelling can be given when the first draft has been completed. Before the teacher reads the writing the children can be encouraged to proofread their own writing, identifying words that they think are incorrectly spelt and either trying to correct these by having another go at the word or searching for the word in a dictionary, or they can indicate the words that they are unsure of by means of a mark. In addition to rereading their own writing pupils can ask another child in the class to read through their work and identify mistakes in the text before it is shown to the teacher. The response partner need not just focus on spelling but may also make suggestions about content, clarity and structure as well. This routine introduces an audience other than the teacher for the children's writing and helps to make writing a collaborative rather than an individual activity. This suggestion fits in with the non-statutory guidance for writing at key stage 1 (NCC, 1990), which states that 'Effective help will start with the children's own work, introducing drafting and opportunities for collaboration, to encourage planning and critical reading.'

Computers and spelling

It has been suggested by Potter and Sands (1988) that children's spelling may improve when they use word processors for writing. They suggest that incorrect spellings are more easily identified when they appear on the screen or on a printout than when they are handwritten. Spellings that are then identified as incorrect can be deleted and replaced more easily with the computer than in a piece of handwritten text. With the computer the whole text does not need to be rewritten: one only needs to remove misspellings and insert the correct versions. Finally they suggest that children are more motivated to produce correct spellings in writing that is produced on the word processor since the printout of text that looks like commercially published texts emphasizes the public nature of writing and the understanding that others will read what has been written. With the possibility of an audience, correct spelling has more significance than it has in private writing.

Using the word-processing facilities of the computer to motivate children to check spellings and to correct spellings quickly, presupposes that children use the computer for first drafts and for redrafting their work after identifying things that they want to change. If the computer is used just to copy out perfectly spelt final versions of writing, the whole piece of writing has to be written out again and the ease of correction that the computer provides is lost along with the incentive it provides to make redrafting less time consuming.

Some teachers feel anxious about introducing drafting and redrafting to young children since they feel it may turn writing into a chore. The use of the computer to produce first and subsequent drafts of writing can lessen this chore since the child does not have to copy out each draft afresh. The computer can certainly reduce emphasis on the transcriptional elements of writing since it automatically produces clearly written text that is easily readable, can make the correction of spellings simple and takes the effort out of redrafting. All this means that the child can be freed to concentrate on the composition of writing and yet still produce a perfectly presented piece of writing.

Spelling checkers provide another source of help for children's spelling. They can enable children to check the spellings of words that they think may be wrong or the programme itself may identify words that are incorrectly spelt in a piece of writing. In order to prevent children from becoming too engrossed with correct spelling at the cost of composition it is suggested that spelling checkers are not used until after the first draft of a piece of writing has been completed. In this way their use could be introduced as one would any source of correct spellings that is available in the classroom.

Dictionaries

The statements of attainment for spelling (DES, 1990) suggest that by level 2 children should be beginning to use dictionaries and that by level 3 children should be beginning to use a simple dictionary or other classroom resources 'to check the accuracy of their spelling'. In the Programme of Study (DES, 1990) the 'other resources' are identified as an alphabetical word bank or a book where they know that the word that they want appears.

Children can be introduced to the use of commercially produced dictionaries by making a large class dictionary to which new words are added when different themes are undertaken by the class. The new vocabulary can be written in by the children to produce a useful resource for the pupils. Making a dictionary gives children a sense of alphabetical order and introduces the idea of looking for spellings in other dictionaries and books that are available in the class.

For younger children, or as an alternative activity to introduce knowledge and understanding of alphabetical order, the children can produce an alphabet frieze or poster. A good starting point for the words on class-made alphabet friezes is the names of the children in the class and the school. Other topics for friezes include food and animals.

Spelling and handwriting

There have been suggestions that introducing young children to cursive script can help with correct spelling. When a writer prints, each letter is isolated from the one before it and the one after it and the hand does not build up a memory for how it feels to produce certain patterns of letters. When letters in words are joined there is an increased possibility that the correct version of a word will be remembered since both the visual and the motor memory are being used. The multi-sensory approach to learning spelling has been advocated as a useful way to support learning for children needing intensive remedial help with spelling (Fernald, 1943) but there is no reason why the principles can not be applied to all children. Peters (1985) suggests that this is particularly helpful for memorizing letter strings such as *ough* or *ight*.

Some children adapt their handwriting to help their spelling on their own initiative. For example, it is quite common to see children use a capital *B* in the middle of a text that is mostly written using lower-case letters. This is often a device for avoiding reversals and distinguishing between letters that are commonly confused. Handwriting corrections of words that are incorrectly spelt because of letter reversals, as with *bog* for *dog*, will improve some children's spelling.

What to correct
Many teachers and parents believe that the process of developmental writing requires no corrections of misspelt words; this is not the case. Correction of spellings is gradual, systematic and should be related to the individual abilities of each child. The example that follows illustrates how to correct some spelling errors in a particular child's work. There are no hard and fast rules; as a teacher with knowledge of individual children's needs and strengths you will make your own judgements about what to correct. It is unlikely that the teacher would just concentrate on spelling when correcting a piece of written work; the focus on spelling that follows has been deliberately constructed to illustrate some of the points made in this chapter.

Stuart aged six (Figure 4.6)
The Ink Well
September the 30th
First of all Mrs Pike brought in a box. We had to guess what it was. We though it was a watch box, a clock box, soap box, jewellery box, a ring box, a valuable box and a radio, but it was not any of these. It was an ink box from the Victorian times.

Context
A visitor came to the school and showed the children a number of antique items. She asked the children to guess what they were used for. After she left, the children were asked to write about one of the items and include all of the guesses that had been made. Stuart chose to write about the travelling ink-well. This was a first draft.

Comment
The spelling in this piece of writing communicates his meaning very clearly and many words are spelt correctly. Stuart also used some of the words on display in the classroom, such as *Victorian* and *times*, to help him with his spelling. He demonstrates that he is aware of spelling patterns by incorporating *ought* into *brought* although he has missed out the *r* in this word. However, he does not use this spelling pattern when spelling *thought*. The misspelling here seems to arise from Stuart's over-reliance on the phonic elements of spelling – the word is spelt very much as he would pronounce it. Stuart made a very good attempt at the word *jewellery*, his spelling *gurliy* again resembles the way it is said. *Vavue* for *valuable* shows Stuart using the visual and phonic aspects of writing. He is aware that *u* and *e* can occur together in words and produce the sound *U*. This piece of writing shows that Stuart is not deterred from attempting words that are difficult to spell. From this piece of writing Stuart seems to be a level 2 speller when assessed using the statements of attainment.

STuarT

The Ink Well
September The 30th
birsht OF all MRs blke
bought In a box. We had
To ges what It Was We
Forelt Wos a Watch box
a CloK box
soap Box Gurliy Box a ring
Box a vavue Box an
rediQ but It Was not
enany oF These
It was an InK Box krom
The victorIan times.

Figure 4.6

What next?

Stuart could be asked to read this piece of work again in order to try and identify any words that he felt were not spelt correctly. I would hope that he might identify *enany*; if he did not, this would be one of the words that I would draw his attention to. It seems as if he began to write this word using *en*, recognized his mistake and began again but forgot to cross out the first two letters. As *radio* is almost correct I would point out the one error in it and ask Stuart to learn this word using the 'look, cover, remember, write, check' system. Finally I might draw Stuart's attention to the correct use of *ought* in *brought* and tell him that this forms part of the word *thought*. Stuart is obviously developing well in spelling and will make progress if he continues to write and is encouraged to think about what words look like. In future Stuart could be reminded to proofread his writing and to look for words that he could correct on his own.

Conclusion

Spelling is a complex skill and children can not be expected to be perfect spellers from the time they begin to write. Indeed to encourage this may emphasize transcription at the cost of content. By providing children with correctly spelt words the teacher denies herself the opportunity to see what children do know about spelling and may inhibit them from making efforts when they are spelling. Spelling does improve as children gain more practice and experience as writers and if they are made aware of the communicative function of writing. At no time should the teacher emphasize the importance of spelling to the detriment of children's desire to communicate through writing. Children do learn to write and spell by writing, so if they are motivated to write and the teacher provides guidance their spelling will improve over time.

Questions about spelling

Q. If children are allowed to write spellings incorrectly, don't they remember the wrong spellings and thus get into bad habits?

A. This is very unlikely. If you use word books think how many times children copy correct versions of words but still can not spell the word without copying or without your help. Think about how many times you look up the same word in the dictionary and copy it out. If spelling were merely about writing the correct version very few children or adults would have any problems.

Q. Some children are excellent readers but have real difficulties with spelling, why is this?

A. Good readers tend to read quickly. They tend to focus on the meaning of a text rather than the details of each word so although they look at the text they do not analyse the letters contained in each word. Reading and spelling are two separate activities: reading is concerned with processing meaning and spelling is about producing meaning. Being able to understand something does not automatically mean that one can produce a similar thing. Good readers may need just as much help with spelling as poor readers.

Q. Does the way children speak affect the way they spell?

A. There is no evidence to suggest that this is a major factor in children's misspellings or that it presents children with problems. When children are at the phonetic stage of searching for sounds to represent the words they write they may use the way they speak to give them clues, for example writing *fing* for *thing*, but this is a temporary phase and as children gain visual experience of words mistakes of this nature diminish.

In the spelling test at the start of the chapter all the words except *parallel* were spelt correctly.

5

Handwriting

Introduction

Within this chapter three aspects of handwriting at school are considered. The first section examines the aims of teaching handwriting. Handwriting style, the subject of the next section, should support the aims of handwriting which are legibility, fluency and speed when writing. The second section also considers the debate about when and how children should be introduced to cursive script. The final section in this chapter is 'How to help with handwriting'. This section contains practical suggestions for helping children with the presentation of their writing. It includes a consideration of resources, teaching strategies, provision for left-handed pupils, and the reasons why parents and carers need to be aware of the school's handwriting policy.

The aims of teaching handwriting

One of the aims of every school's English policy should be to teach children to write legibly, fluently and with reasonable speed. As with spelling, handwriting forms a separate attainment target in the English National Curriculum and this is a reminder that handwriting is only one part of the overall writing process. While clear writing is the goal, handwriting practice is the servant not the master of writing. As the non-statutory guidance (NCC, 1990) states, 'Teachers should appreciate that overemphasis on formation is not effective and can damage confidence.' Clear, well-formed handwriting does not develop naturally, it needs to be taught carefully and sensitively so that all children are helped to form and join letters quickly, easily and legibly.

Since the purpose of all writing is to communicate, the writer needs to do this easily and the recipient of the writing needs to understand the message easily. Clear, quickly formed handwriting aids this act of communication. Thus it is important that handwriting is legible.

Fluency in writing means that the writer is at ease with the writing system and with writing implements, pencil or pen grip is firm but not tense and the letters are correctly formed. It has been suggested by Peters (1985) that fluency can help the writer with spelling. Spelling patterns or groups of letters that are frequently found together in words can be written almost automatically. For example, *a n d* are often found together. The fluent writer hardly needs to pause as she writes this group of letters. Such automatic production of letters can aid spelling if the writer can form the letters correctly and efficiently. Those who consider that spelling is aided by a kinaesthetic approach suggest that a cursive script is taught from the beginning, giving children the mechanics that enable them to join up letter strings and develop a 'feel' for word shapes and letter strings.

Speed and fluency go together: if the child knows how to form letters she will form them quickly. The main reason that 'infant script' is thought of as the 'correct' method of letter formation for young children is that it is an economical and legible style and for the most part leaves the pen in the appropriate place for a joining stroke when cursive script is introduced. Infant script is quick in itself and prepares the writer for faster writing when she begins to join letters.

Handwriting style

Many models of handwriting exist for use in school and most are accompanied by manuals that give teachers information about letter formation and the development of good handwriting. Schools may have individual preferences about the style they choose. The important point is that one style is taught and modelled consistently throughout the school.

The debate about whether cursive script should be introduced to children as soon as they begin to write at school has been with us for many years. Joined-up writing has been viewed as a progression from preliterate patterns (Jarman, 1979), as an aid to spelling (Peters, 1985), as a means of maintaining the flow when writing creatively (Graves, 1983) and as a way of offering young writers models of what they are aiming for from the start of their writing career at school (Cotton, 1991). However, it is only recently that the issue has been discussed seriously in many schools.

The statement of attainment for handwriting at level 3 (DES, 1990) which states that 'pupils should be able to begin to produce clear and legible joined-up writing', has renewed the debate about handwriting styles in first schools and widened its scope from the selection and merits of various forms of print script to include a discussion about print versus cursive script. Unless joined-up handwriting is introduced to children before the age of seven they will not be able to attain level 3 in handwriting, so some teachers have felt that they may be disadvantaging pupils if they do not introduce them to cursive script much earlier than has traditionally been the case.

A question that is often asked that is central to this debate is, 'Is joined-up writing compatible with a developmental approach to writing?' In some ways it may be seen as incompatible. When children first begin to write they often produce capital letters, then a mixture of capital and lower-case letters and finally lower-case with the correct use of capitals. To expect children to move from the pre-literate marks on paper to joined-up writing would exclude the other stages that children go through as they are learning about the writing system. The use of capitals plays a part in spelling development when children use letter names to help them write words. As the typeface in children's books is usually print script, to introduce joined-up writing from the start would seem to be at variance with the models children see and the materials teachers use to teach children lessons about writing. Additionally it might be unwise to expect children to produce joined-up writing before they can form letters correctly. If we were to do this, children might begin to join letters in the wrong places, perhaps from the top rather than the bottom of the letter forms.

What seems to be a possible way forward in this debate is to introduce children to letters with exit strokes from the start, as is suggested by Sassoon (1990). Letters that are made in this way retain the print form similar to that found in books, give children the opportunity to absorb and use correct letter formation and yet provide a model for the flowing movement that develops easily into joins. With this style children need only extend and speed up these exit strokes to form joins as their handwriting matures. The following example shows how this might work. The child writes *HOM*. The teacher writes the correct spelling next to the word using print with integral baseline exit strokes as in *home.*This way the child is presented with a model that will join easily when the child is ready.

If schools prefer to teach a traditional form of infant script to younger children and joined writing to older children the order of introduction might be as follows:

- Beginning writers – print script.
- Children using lower-case print confidently with only a few incorrectly formed letters – introduce joined letter strings when modelling or discussing children's spelling.
- Children using lower-case print well and forming letters correctly –

begin to introduce them to joining letters when it is comfortable and quicker for them.

This sequence implies that joined writing would be introduced as the individual child showed herself ready to incorporate it into her writing. The majority of children should begin to reach this stage by their third year at school.

Figure 5.1

It is important that whole-school decisions are taken about the style of handwriting adopted and how it is taught in order to ensure continuity and progression as children develop as writers and as they move through the school. All the teachers in the school need to be aware of the style of handwriting chosen by the school and to be able to match their writing to this when writing for displays and providing models for children as well as for teaching.

How to help with handwriting

The teacher's role when teaching handwriting is to provide the appropriate resources which children need to practise the skill and to demonstrate to children how letters and words should be formed. Correction and demonstration should arise from how the child writes. The purpose of well-presented and correctly formed writing should always be explained to children so that they understand the reasons for attending to the skills of writing.

Sassoon (1990) writes that thick pencils are not necessarily helpful for small infant fingers and suggests that a variety of writing implements should be made available to children. A range of writing implements can make writing more interesting and should include different sizes of pencils, fibre-tipped pens, felt-tips, wax crayons and pencil crayons. These should be available for children to choose from. It might be appropriate to encourage children to use pencils for first drafts of writing and pens or felt-tips for second drafts. The type of paper used may influence the choice of writing implement.

Traditionally, beginning writers have used unlined paper to write on. Young children may have problems keeping to lines. They are not always sure which part of a letter rests on the line and may place the tails of letters such as *p* and *g* on the lines if given lined paper too quickly. Unlined paper seems to give children the freedom to experiment with letter formation and size as well as giving children the flexibility to draw and write. Drawing can be an important part of the writing process since it can be used as a planning strategy by young children. Whilst they draw their picture they can think about what they want to write and how to write this. As children begin to use smaller writing and to form letters correctly they can be introduced to line guides to help keep writing straight across the page. Line guides are made from strong white card with bold black lines drawn at the desired width. The guides are placed beneath the child's writing paper and can be kept in place by paper clips. The lines show through and provide a guide for writing. These have the advantage over lined paper of allowing children freedom to illustrate their writing and to choose where to put their illustrations. It is also a good idea to have different shapes, sizes and colours of paper available for children to stimulate their writing.

It is likely that teachers will have available in the classroom commercial or pupil-made alphabet friezes that children can refer to when writing. Sassoon (1990) suggests that each child could also have available an alphabet strip that she could place on the desk when writing. This might help children to learn the order of the alphabet and help children to sort out which way letters face. It also reminds children of the writing style that the school favours.

Handwriting is a skill that needs to be nurtured in the classroom and taught individually to pupils. General provision for fostering good presentation of work will grow from the use of materials and engagement in all the activities that are concerned with artistic, creative and physical education at school. Whitehead (1990) suggests that the skills necessary for handwriting – hand and eye co-ordination, muscle control and visual sensitivity – develop through play activities, art activities and exposure to displays and writing that children see in school. Handwriting can be practised in all areas of the curriculum, for example in art children can produce patterns using letters, print with letter shapes and produce patterns when finger painting. To extend play activities children can make labels for the home corner, shop or office. They can also make labels for their models, giving the name of the model, their own name and a message, as in 'A model house by Shippu and Maria-Elena. Do not touch.'

Handwriting itself is best taught individually to pupils through the writing that they produce rather than through class writing lessons involving copying from the board or from cards. In order to help children improve at handwriting it is best to observe them while they are writing. While observing writing, look for the ease with which the child holds the pen and correct letter formation. The aim is for children to start in the right place and move in the right direction. This is more important than the final letters produced. Problems with handwriting can lead to tense and uncomfortable posture and grip, reluctance to write, slow writing and difficulties with cursive script. Suggestions for correction should only be made about one or at the most two mistakes in one piece of writing and the teacher should focus on poorly formed letters or incorrect joining strokes. Having identified the errors that will be discussed with the child, the teacher may demonstrate the correct formation of these letters and ask the child to practise making them correctly. The child may be asked to produce a line of correctly formed letters and then to rewrite the word in which the mistake occurred. It is not necessary to correct all writing: for example a child's own first draft that is seen primarily by the child may need only to be legible to the child. At no time should children be given the impression that perfectly formed writing is more important than content. Children should be told that good handwriting helps the reader to read what has been written and helps the writer write more quickly. In the non-statutory guidance for handwriting (NCC, 1990, p. B8) the suggestion is that 'Handwriting practice should be purposeful. When there is a purpose and an audience for the writing pupils will appreciate the need for high quality presentation of work of which they can be proud.'

When teachers write underneath children's writing in the early stages of developmental writing or when they work with children on spelling corrections or in sessions involving shared writing, they should make sure that their writing provides a good model for children. They should ensure that children have the opportunity to see well-formed, clear handwriting as it is produced. Good models provide examples that children can see and imitate. In time each writer will develop her own personal style of writing and this need not be a problem. There is nothing wrong with a personal style as long as it is legible, fluent and economic.

Left-handed writers

Left-handers may have particular difficulties with handwriting. It may help if teachers consider the following points:

- Light – ideally a left-hander needs the light to come over her right shoulder so that she is not writing in the shadow of her own hand.
- Paper – a left-hander needs to have paper on the left side of the centre of the body. The paper needs to be tilted to the right so that the writer can see what she is writing.
- Pencil hold – encourage a left-handed writer to hold the pencil or pen a little further from the point than a right-hander so that the writing is not obscured. It may be helpful to introduce children to a pencil grip to find the right place for their fingers.
- Position – make sure that a left-hander is not sitting too close to the right of a right-hander when writing. This will avoid their arms colliding.
- Speed – allow for slower writing until competence increases.
- Teaching – demonstrate to left-handers with your left hand whenever possible.

Most schools now have at least one computer. Word-processing programmes or facilities are an ideal way of varying the writing process. Computers are often a way of motivating children to write and to correct their work using the editing procedures. They can speed up the process of producing first and second drafts of written work. The non-statutory guidance for spelling suggests that text-handling programmes with graphics and a choice of fonts can be used to 'motivate even the least confident writer' (NCC, 1990). Typed script can be an excellent way of producing public documents such as class books. The writing area in the classroom may have an old typewriter for the children to use. More polished writing can be typed out for others to read or children can just enjoy experimenting with writing in this way.

If children's written work is sent home it is a good idea if parents and other adults understand the school policy on handwriting. Make sure that they know that handwriting develops over time and with practice at writing, that it is content that is valued first and that good handwriting is merely a way of making the message clear. Adults may have memories of their own schooldays which lead them to believe that neatness is the prime objective for acceptable written work. They may remember comments such as 'writing needs to be neater' or 'must try harder with presentation'. One of the reasons that teachers may stress neatness to children is because they know that parents look for this when reading children's writing. If this cycle of emphasis on presentation rather than content is to be broken, explanations about writing need to be given to parents.

Teachers might stress to parents and carers the importance of not criticizing children's efforts. Children can be helped at home by having opportunities to experiment in a variety of ways. They can benefit from having access to paper and a variety of writing implements and from encouragement to write.

Conclusion

Handwriting is a skill that needs to be taught. Teachers need to teach children how to produce legible, fluent and swift handwriting and need to explain why this is important. Not every piece of writing that children produce needs to look perfect but teachers should use the writing that children produce to demonstrate correct ways of forming letters and words. There is no need for isolated handwriting practice. The skills of writing, such as handwriting and spelling, do not always transfer if they are isolated from real writing situations. Children learn best if they are given real reasons for making their handwriting legible through having a real audience and a real purpose for writing and if they receive sensitive intervention linked to the writing that they do.

Questions about handwriting

Q. Do children need to have periods of handwriting practice?
A. Whole-class handwriting sessions seem to have little value when teaching handwriting. Even if a particular style of handwriting is used, formal exercises are not an essential accompaniment to this. During class handwriting sessions it is not usually possible to observe whether children are forming their letters correctly and a piece of writing can result that looks good but that conceals errors. In addition, there seems to be very little transfer from handwriting practice to how children write at other times. Instead it seems good practice to fit the teaching of handwriting to individual children's needs and to correct errors with the child

as one observes them occurring in everyday writing. Each child's needs will be different. The best time to emphasize careful presentation of written work is probably just before the child is making a final draft of her work when corrections that have been made should be included. It is at this time that children can see the point of making writing legible and attractive since others may read what has been written.

Q. Is Biro a suitable medium for writing in school?

A. Biro can look messy so it is probably not a good tool for a final best draft but it can be used for rough work. Teachers may like to put a Biro in the home corner for children to use there since many children will be familiar with Biros at home. If children do not use rubbers when writing first drafts they can write in any medium as long as it is legible. For final drafts, where presentation is important, roller-ball pens or fountain pens give a professional finish to written work.

Q. When should pens be introduced to children?

A. Pens, as the implements that are used for a best copy, should be introduced to children as soon as they start school. It is likely that most children will have had experience of using pens before they come to school so they should be quite familiar with their use.

Q. Most girls seem to write neatly and many boys are untidy. Why is this?

A. It is true that some girls can spend a long time producing a few lines of perfectly formed writing whereas boys can produce writing that is often longer but that shows little regard for presentation. This may be because girls are often expected to be neat and are praised for their tidiness. In writing, the teacher can address this issue by making sure that girls understand that they can use a rough draft in any way that they want to and by emphasizing that initially content is more important than presentation in writing. The teacher may also want to make it clear to children who are habitually untidy that careless final drafts are unacceptable, even if the content is good, since they are difficult for others to read.

6

Assessment and Record-Keeping

Introduction

This chapter is divided into two sections. The first section, 'The nature of assessment', offers a definition of assessment, presents a synopsis of the current statutory requirements and a summary of the principles of assessment. Using the legislation and the principles as guidelines, the second section, 'Assessment and writing', considers the role of assessment in the teaching of writing. It looks at what should be assessed and offers suggestions about how to assess children's writing. It considers how assessment in writing can inform teaching, contribute to an effective form of record-keeping and fulfil current legislative demands.

The nature of assessment

Assessment is a vital part of the curriculum that is presented to children at school. It is the evaluation of what has been learned by the pupils and of what has been planned and implemented by the teacher. 'Assessment lies at the heart' of the process of promoting children's learning and it is this that is the 'principle aim of schools' (DES, 1988, p. 000). Assessment can enhance learning since, by collecting information and evidence about children's achievements and experiences and by analysing these to see what has been learnt and how it has been learnt, the teacher may gain greater understanding of how children learn and be able to match her planning and teaching closely to the learning needs of children.

Assessment can be formative or summative. Formative assessment occurs throughout a period of learning. During this time the teacher is concerned with collecting information about the progress and needs of the pupils. She is able to see what they can do and what they need to do next. Summative assessment records the achievements of pupils in a systematic way at the end of a phase of learning, for example at the end of key stage 1. In order to make accurate judgements about children at the end of a phase of learning the teacher will consider the range of evidence that has been collected throughout the phase. Both formative and summative assessment are important since in both cases teachers will be able to use the outcomes in order to plan and accommodate the future learning needs of children. Information about the process of learning and the outcomes of learning can lead to greater understanding of the learning process and this can lead to changes and improvements in teaching.

In 1988 the Education Reform Act established that assessments for each of the core and foundation subjects in the National Curriculum would occur at or near the end of each key stage (HM Government, 1988). These arrangements included not only the standard assessment tasks (SATs) but also the teachers' assessments of children's levels of attainment. It was expected that teacher assessments would be supported by the evidence that had been collected by teachers throughout a phase of learning. In 1989 governing bodies of schools were required by the Education (School Records) Regulations to ensure that schools maintained annually updated records on all registered pupils. These records were expected to contain evidence of academic and other achievements and to show the progress that each pupil had made in school. It was further stated that these records were to be available to entitled and responsible people as defined by the regulations.

One of the most recent publications from the National Curriculum Council, *Starting out with the National Curriculum* (NCC, 1992), outlines the assessment, recording and reporting procedures that are expected of schools. It identifies assessment as 'a central feature of the National Curriculum' (p. 000) and defines assessment as a combination of the results of nationally set tasks or tests and teacher assessment.

This document clearly identifies some of the key features of teacher assessment. These include:

- **Using professional Judgement**: teachers are encouraged to refine their professional judgements through moderation and discussion with other teachers; it is suggested that the examination of pupils' work with others will be part of this discussion process.
- **Involving pupils in their own assessment**: pupils should be actively involved in reviewing their own work and deciding in discussion with teachers which pieces of work provide evidence of particular attainments.
- **Recording attainment**: a record of each child's achievements in relation to the attainment targets, statements of attainment and end-of-key-stage statements should be kept.
- **Collecting evidence**: evidence of attainments in the form of samples

of work and observations should be collected. The document states that it is 'important to be able to point to examples of achievement which support particular judgements . . . Collections of work with teacher's notes can be particularly useful'.

- **Reporting to parents**: this section suggests that the knowledge that teachers build up about pupils through teacher assessment can help to make reports useful to parents; also that parents should be involved in their children's learning.

When considering the best ways of assessing progress and achievement it is useful to examine what constitutes good practice in assessment. Listed below are six principles of assessment that may influence the way in which teachers decide to carry out assessment in school.

Assessment should be fair

To ensure fairness there should be explicit criteria and standards that are used to determine quality. These may be drawn up in relation to the stages of development that have been identified with regard to writing and in addition may be related to the objective statements of attainment as described in the statutory orders of the National Curriculum for English (DES, 1990). As a further control of fairness multiple measures of assessment should be used. These may include evidence from a number of sources, such as samples of work over time and observations from a variety of people.

Assessment should be valid

For assessment to be valid there needs to be a clear relationship between the process of evaluation and what it claims to describe. So if one is assessing content and organization of a piece of writing the context of the work should make this clear and possible. There should also be procedures for determining the validity of interpretations and this means that the evidence on which one has based one's judgements should be available for others to see.

Assessment should be relevant

The material and information collected during the process of assessment should be directly related to the criteria used in the decision process and the needs of the decision-makers. So when assessing writing it is necessary to have samples of writing that are drawn from a variety of starting points and demonstrate the various aspects of writing that are to be assessed.

Assessment should be useful
Both the process and the product of assessment should be useful to those who are assessed and to the assessors; the information that is gained from assessment should be fed back into the teaching and learning process and this should help both the pupil and the teacher.

Assessment should be multidimensional
What is being assessed needs to be set in context. When a piece of writing is being assessed this context includes how the writing arose, what the writing was for and the child's previous experience, ability and attitude. To be truly multidimensional there should be multiple methods of data collection and analysis and a number of individuals should be involved in the process.

Assessment should support development
Assessment should never damage or threaten individuals, either the teacher or the learner; instead it should be used to improve practice and achievement.

The guidelines offered by the NCC and the principles of assessment seem a good place to start when thinking about what and how to assess at school. It is clear from these that detailed records of assessment should be kept if assessment is to be fair, valid, useful and multidimensional. It is also clear that assessment should be useful to the teacher. The results of assessment may be used to inform her own practice and to help her when reporting to others on the progress that children have made.

Assessment and writing

The use and understanding of assessment and record-keeping in school have changed considerably over the past few years. The National Curriculum and the standard assessment tasks for seven-year-olds have made assessment and record-keeping a requirement of every teacher's daily work in the classroom. In 1990 HMI wrote,

> In future there will be a demand for far greater attention in many schools to be paid to assessing, recording and reporting children's progress in language and literacy. The information yielded from these assessments will be crucial for the purposes of planning, monitoring progress in the work, and communicating children's progress to parents and others. (HMI, 1990, p. 33)

The first aim of assessment in writing is to discover the competence, understanding and skills that the child has as a writer. The role of the teacher is to develop children's writing, to help children enjoy writing and to enable children to discover personal reasons for writing. In order to do this effectively she has to establish what children can do and what they need to be able to do next. The child's needs will change over time and will be related to the teacher's aims and the child's experience with writing. The teacher will also use assessment to give feedback to children about their writing, including their successes and their difficulties. The explanations and the information that are given to children may help to clarify aspects of the writing process for them and will probably form an important part of the teaching and learning process. Teachers also assess so that they are in a position to comment on children's progress to parents and carers and other interested adults such as the child's next teacher or school governors. Finally, teachers have to undertake assessments in order to make judgements on children's achievements in line with the requirements of the National Curriculum. In order to achieve all these aims it is necessary not only to examine children's writing but also to look at the classroom practices that support children's learning. Whenever learning is assessed teaching is also scrutinized to see what and how far the teaching has enabled the learner to learn.

What is assessed is linked to what has been taught and the teacher's expectations about how children learn to write. It is likely that it will cover the areas of writing, spelling and handwriting as they are expressed for English in the National Curriculum (NCC, 1990). An important factor in children's writing development is their attitude to writing since this may affect their willingness to learn about the conventions of writing and to spend time and effort on their writing.

The information received from regular assessment gives teachers insights into the children and their learning and into how well the teaching is being received. All assessment of learning involves a corresponding reflection on teaching to see if the curriculum, presentation and organization provide an appropriate environment for learning for all pupils. The questions that follow might provide a helpful framework for examining and reflecting on both these aspects. They provide a checklist of things to look out for when assessing children's writing through analysing samples, observing pupils, discussions with children and when involving pupils in their own assessment.

Attitudes

About the child
1 What is the child's attitude to writing?
2 Can the child see her own reasons for writing?
3 Does the child choose to write freely?

4 Is the child involved in her writing and does she sustain that involvement over time?

About my practice
1 Am I an enthusiastic writer?
2 Do I convey this enthusiasm to my pupils?
3 Do I provide a range of resources for writing for the children?
4 Do I make provision for writing in play activities?
5 Do I give children a variety of written activities with different purposes and audiences?
6 What happens to finished writing? Is it praised, displayed, published or shared with others?

Content

About the child
1 Are the ideas expressed in writing equivalent or nearly equivalent to those expressed orally?
2 Does the child use vivid, imaginative and appropriate language in her writing?
3 Does the child organize her writing clearly?
4 Can the child write in a variety of styles and formats?
5 Which styles does the child find easiest?

About my practice
1 Do I respond to content and organization first when assessing children's writing?
2 Are a range of writing styles and formats displayed around the classroom?
3 Do I encourage children to 'have a go' at difficult or unusual spellings?
4 Have I given children strategies for collecting ideas for pieces of written work, for example brainstorming, listing, etc.?
5 Do I give guidance on ways of organizing and planning written work using drawings, diagrams, headings, etc.?
6 Do I demonstrate all the processes involved in writing through shared-writing sessions?
7 Do I encourage children to discuss stories and to base some of their writing on familiar story structures?

Writing conventions

About the child
1 Does the child use visual and phonic strategies when spelling?
2 Does the child make use of capital letters, full stops and speech marks in her writing?

3 Is the child's writing clear and legible?
4 Does the child use grammatically appropriate structures in her writing, for example sustaining the use of *he* throughout a narrative written in the third person?

About my practice
1 Do I encourage children to look at and memorize words as part of my spelling policy?
2 Do I encourage children to notice grammatical features in books that they are sharing with the teacher or reading alone?
3 Do I correct handwriting errors in the presence of the child?
4 Do I encourage children to reread their writing once it is finished?

Teachers carry out assessment in two ways: first, the frequent formative assessment of children's progress as they are writing; and, second, more formal assessments that are made at the end of a year or a phase of learning.

Formative assessment usually takes place during the course of a writing activity. It is an integral part of the child's learning about writing rather than something separate. As part of the regular assessment process, teachers will use a variety of methods, including analysis of the child's writing, both as she writes and after a piece of writing has been completed, observation of the child as she writes, and discussion with the child about her writing. She may also involve the child in the assessment process. These four methods are important parts of the assessment procedure since they provide insights into the process of writing as well as the outcome of the activity. It is important to look at how the child sets about the task as well as what the child can do in order to extend her understanding as well as her skills. It is also useful to see what the child can do in a variety of contexts as this may vary.

When it is time to make a summative assessment of a child's learning the teacher will need to refer to all the sources of evidence that have been collected during a phase of learning if the assessment is to be fair and multidimensional. These will include samples of writing, written observations of pupils, notes of interactions with pupils, children's own assessments of their writing, and information provided by others such as parents, carers and other teachers. The records may also contain photographs of work and a list of the topics and themes undertaken each year by each child. In addition they may contain a note of the National Curriculum attainment target levels reached by the child and a copy of the school report issued to parents or carers each year. For those children who have taken the SATs teachers might include the SAT levels and the work that the children undertook for them.

Record-keeping is a way of preserving the assessments that teachers make about children's learning and making the basis for such assessments available to others in a tangible and clear form. Circular 12/92 from the Department for Education suggests that in order to do this effectively each school must have a policy in place to 'gather systematically, record and review evidence of each pupil's attainment in relation to the statutory attainment targets throughout key stage 1 (DFE, 1992). As part of this policy, schools are expected to have records containing 'evidence of pupil attainment which can be readily passed from teacher to teacher'.

Assessing writing and keeping records of a child's development in writing are relatively straightforward since writing is easily collected and once collected can be analysed and assessed at the teacher's leisure. The evidence that the writing samples provide about the child's development and needs as a learner is tangible and permanent and can be a useful starting point for discussion with the child or with parents. The writing that is collected and analysed will provide the basis of the child's writing profile. In addition to the samples of writing, the profile will contain observations, records of interactions with the child, the child's own assessments of her writing and any comments from parents, carers and other teachers about the child as a writer. The rest of this section looks at the different ways of assessing children's writing and children as writers and examines what teachers may learn from these different methods of assessment.

Analysing samples of writing

One way of gaining insights into a child's writing development is to analyse what the child writes. This is done frequently when the child brings a piece of writing to the teacher to look at. As the teacher reads the writing she is analysing it, noting what the child has done and how she has done it. Keeping samples of writing over time and analysing them at leisure provides even more insights into the child's progress as a writer. If the teacher is able to recognize points of growth signified in the writing and to see improvements over previous work the analysis will be more useful in understanding the child's needs as a writer and planning future work. The teacher may also use the child's work as a starting point for a discussion and further exploration with the child.

Not every piece of writing that a child completes needs to be included in her writing record. The teacher may choose to include two or three samples each term. It is useful to include one piece of writing from the beginning of the school year as this provides a baseline from which teaching can proceed. This also provides a reference point when assessing how much progress children have made over the course of a term or a year. The rest of the samples that are included should show progress and be drawn from a variety of starting points and curriculum areas and represent a variety of styles of writing, for example factual, imaginative, descriptive and chronological. First drafts as well as fair copies should be included to show how the child revises and corrects her work as well as how she has responded to suggestions from the teacher. Some of the writing may be selected by the child, for example her best piece of writing each term. The child's comments about these pieces of writing should be recorded and accompany the sample.

Once a piece of work has been selected it should be dated and then analysed. The following headings may be useful when examining writing:

- **Context**: This section might include notes about how the work arose, the purpose of the writing, the intended audience, the length of time the child spent on the writing and information about the child's previous knowledge or experience in this area.
- **Comment**: This section is concerned with the strengths and weaknesses displayed by the child as a writer. Here one might consider what the writing shows about the child as a learner. The comments may refer to attitude, content and writing conventions as displayed in the piece of work. If plans and drafts are collected, one might note the differences between the drafts and the learning processes that the child has gone through by comparing first and final copies. When examining pupils' written work it may be useful to look for positive points and points of growth and to ask oneself, 'What has the child attempted and achieved?'
- **Attainment targets**: A note could be made here of the attainment targets covered or reached in this piece of work. Although the primary focus might be on the attainment targets for English, the piece of writing could have arisen from another area of the curriculum and demonstrate learning that meets attainment targets from other curriculum areas.
- **What next?**: The teacher might indicate in this section the activities, experiences and work that might extend the child as a learner.

Figure 6.1 and 6.2 show two samples of writing from a six-year-old pupil, Imran, that show development over time. Imran's first language was Urdu but at the time of this writing he was able to talk clearly in English. He enjoyed writing but tended to rush at his work.

Figure 6.1

Imran, aged six (Figure 6.1)

Context
This piece of writing emerged after the children had listened to the story *William's Doll* (Zolotow, 1972). The children had been asked to think about the sorts of games that both girls and boys like to play.

Comment
Imran writes easily and confidently. He always uses the same letters when he is writing. He does not yet see the connection between sounds and words that he writes. He was able to read back what he had written and the teacher wrote the correct version close to his words. Imran and the teacher talked about the letters that were common to both sets of writing. The teacher also talked to Imran about spaces between words.

Attainment targets
This piece of work indicates that Imran is currently achieving level 1 in writing and handwriting and working towards level 1 in spelling.

What next?
Imran needs to be encouraged to think before he writes. He needs to consider the initial letters of words and to learn the sounds and names of letters. Work on these aspects during shared reading and shared writing will help. He needs to continue to gain practice at writing and to be praised for his positive approach to writing.

Figure 6.2

Imran, aged six (Figure 6.2)
How I made my home
First we got a box
Then we cut the door
Then we put the carpet
Then I me and Kevin finished.

Context
The children were working on the theme of 'homes' and after listening to the story *Charlie's House* (Schermbruker and Daly, 1992) had worked in pairs to make a home for Charlie. The writing was an account of how they had made the home. The children were going to copy out their writing to make explanatory notes for the display of model houses. The title was written on a flip chart for the children to copy.

Comment
This writing demonstrates a vast improvement since September. The writing is well constructed, there are spaces between words, many of the spellings approximate closely to the correct versions, some words are correctly spelt, such as *we, door* and *put*, there is evidence of attention to initial letter sounds and a greater variety of letters.

Attainment targets
This piece of writing shows that Imran is now reaching level 2b in the statements of attainment for writing, levels 2a, 2b, 2c and 2d in spelling, and level 1 in handwriting.

What next?
Imran needs to continue gaining experience as a reader and a writer. The teacher needs to continue to draw his attention to the details of print, including the use of upper- and lower-case letters in text, and may begin to show Imran how to proofread his writing before he brings it to her.

Observation
Observation involves listening to and watching pupils engaged in an activity. Sometimes observations will be preplanned, having a specific focus identified earlier by the teacher, or they may occur routinely as she moves around the classroom checking on children's engagement with the task. Children should be observed as frequently as possible when writing. Although teachers continually make observations about children's work and progress in the course of daily classroom

activities, all children may not be observed equally. For example, quiet children may have less teacher attention than children who have difficulties or those who frequently seek the teacher's help. To ensure that all children are observed over a period, it might be necessary to draw up a schedule of observations. For instance, teachers may decide to observe one writing activity that will be undertaken by all the children in the class over the course of a few days. The teacher will focus on each group of children as they work at this writing activity. Alternatively the teacher might identify two or three children to observe each day until all the class have been observed as they write. In addition, there may be spontaneous and important moments of literacy learning that occur and that are observed. These may represent a significant step in the learning development of a particular child. These too may be noted or recorded by the teacher. It may be useful for the teacher to have a loose-leaf notebook that can be used as a diary of observations. Several pages can be allocated to each child in the class and as they are completed they can be removed, analysed and placed in the child's record folder.

If the child is biliterate or comes from a home where the majority of print is likely to be in a script other than English it is useful to observe her progress in her home language as well as in English since she may be writing and learning about writing but expressing this in her home language. If the child writes freely in her heritage language and understands the purpose of writing, her attitude and understanding are important and contribute to the teacher's overall picture of the child as a writer. One would also expect these to transfer to her writing in English as she becomes more experienced in its use and forms. Knowledge of a first language supports the acquisition of a second language if children are encouraged to use such knowledge. 'Awareness of writing in any form can help pupils to understand some of the functions of written language and should be used to promote understanding of the functions of the English writing system' (Programme of Study for writing, spelling and handwriting for key stage 1, DES, 1990).

One or two observations for each pupil should be recorded each term. As observations are recorded, a picture of the child's development as a writer will be built up. If teachers look back on these observations they will be able to draw conclusions about the development the child has made and the support she needs.

Below are two examples of observations featuring two Year two children. Each observation has been analysed to show the value of observational data in adding to one's picture of the child as a learner and in providing evidence for teacher assessments.

2/11/92   John
Tiny writing.
Does not use the page correctly.
Crosses out continually. Can only guess at first letters of words. Little knowl-edge of letter patterns. Words he knows: the, and, we, put. *Common mis-takes:* soc *for* stories. *Does not know letter names. Reverses* b *and* d. *Can form letters correctly.*
Doesn't want to write.
Finds it difficult to make the words make sense. Panics about work.
Chooses because of difficulties to talk and not complete work.
Needs more opportunities to write for a purpose – short texts.

Commentary
From this observation it is clear that John is having difficulties with writing and because he finds it difficult he does not want to write. The teacher needs to find ways of making writing easier for John. If he is to make progress as a writer he needs to become interested in writing. He needs to establish his own reasons for writing. The observation also indicates that some direct teaching of how to form *b* and *d* would be useful. Without this observation it might have been easy for an adult to think that John was having problems with forming all his letters correctly since the *b* and the *d* are reversed but the evidence is that these are the only two letters that present problems. The teacher might also begin to revise letter names with him and provide some activities that encourage John to look at how words are spelt. He needs to see how writers use the page and how writing is arranged.

The observation provides some of the evidence needed to show that John is reaching level 1c and level 2b of the statements of attainment for spelling. These state that 'Pupils should be able to: use at least single letters or groups of letters to represent whole words or parts of words' and 'spell correctly, in the course of their own writing, simple monosyl-labic words they use regularly which observe common patterns' (DES, 1990). In handwriting the observation suggests that John is working towards level 2 with its emphasis on correctly formed letters.

The following observation, although primarily about Glen, also features John and gives further information about him as a writer when he is working collaboratively with a more able and enthusiastic child.

12/11/92   Glen and John
Glen asked if he could make a book about Mrs Plug the Plumber (Ahlberg, 1980). *Chose John to work with him.*
He has now been working on the book for two days.

13/11/92
Glen and John read the book to the class today. They are extraordinarily proud of it.
Glen explained how they worked – planning together, writing a first draft together and then each writing a page of the final draft in turn. They also took turns with the illustrations. They needed to refer to the text to remind themselves of the details of the story.
They worked without any help from me on this project.

Commentary
Although John has many difficulties with writing, he is able to sustain his interest in writing when he is supported by a more able writer. Glen is able to work independently for long periods of time and is willing to collaborate with others.

The second observation includes evidence of Glen reaching the following statements of attainment for writing: level 3c – 'write more complex stories with detail beyond simple events and with a defined ending; level 3e – 'begin to revise and redraft in discussion with the teacher, other adults, or other children in the class, paying attention to meaning and clarity as well as checking for matters such as correct and consistent use of tenses and pronouns' (DES, 1990).

The second extract also shows how the work that the children have done fulfils the requirements of the Programme of Study for writing at key stage 1 (DES, 1990), statements 10 and 14. They have been engaged in writing together, 'sharing their writing with others and discussing what they have written', and have produced 'finished pieces of work for wider audiences', in this case a book for themselves and other children to share. They have also recognized that writing involves 'decision-making', 'planning' and 'drafting'.

Although these are primarily observations of children writing, they also contain evidence of achievement in speaking and listening and reading. The teacher has seen both children 'participate as speakers and listeners in a group engaged in a given task', 'describe an event, real or imagined, to the teacher or another pupil' and, in order to complete the task, 'listen attentively to stories . . . and talk about them'. These are the statements of attainment for speaking and listening, level 2a, level 2b and level 2c. In terms of the National Curriculum requirements for reading both children have shown that they can 'read a range of material with some independence, fluency, accuracy and understanding' (level 2f), listen attentively to stories, talk about setting, story-line and characters and recall significant details' (level 3c) and 'bring to their writing and discussion about stories some understanding of the way stories are structured' (level 3).

The two observations provide a rich picture of both children's strengths, weaknesses and learning styles. They provide the teacher with important information that could be missed if the teacher only referred to samples of work for her assessments. Reflection on the observation gives the teacher an indication of what to work on next with both children in order to meet their individual needs as developing writers.

Interactions with children

Interaction occurs when teachers talk to pupils about their work. They can take place frequently as the teacher supports the child's writing through writing conferences or normal classroom interaction and less frequently through a lengthy writing interview held once or twice each term with each pupil in the class. Discussions between teachers and pupils about writing may provide opportunities for children to reflect on their learning and enable the teacher to share her observations with pupils. In this form of assessment the teacher will be asking questions and listening carefully to answers. She may be drawing out ideas and checking understanding. There may be a specific focus for the discussion that enables the teacher to check her observations or to explore an aspect of the child's writing behaviour more thoroughly. The non-statutory guidance for writing (NCC, 1990, p. E5) suggests that through discussion with children, 'teachers can find out what they are planning and drafting in a piece of writing . . . the children can talk . . . about the organisation of their writing. This enables the teacher to discuss drafting . . . vocabulary, spelling and punctuation.' If some of the comments a child makes during a writing conference or in response to the teacher's comments are recorded by the teacher these can be added to the child's writing profile, either as an indication of the child's general writing strategies or, if attached to the particular piece of writing to which they refer, they may supplement the teacher's own analysis of the writing. The comments may provide further evidence for the child achieving statements of attainment for writing.

Children's assessment of writing

Involving pupils in the assessment process helps them to reflect on and understand what they have learnt. Children can be asked to review and comment on their learning experiences and their own development as writers. Children can be involved in their own assessment in a systematic way when the teacher is reviewing the child's writing profile. She may ask the child to select an additional piece of writing, from that completed during the term, to be included or she may ask the child to comment on one or all of the pieces of writing that she has selected for inclusion. As the child talks about the writing the teacher should note down what she says and include this with the piece of writing that was discussed. The English non-statutory guidance (NCC, 1990, p. E7) suggests that 'pupils should be involved in the selection of work for a coursework folder'. The child may talk about her perception of herself as a writer and what she might like to do next in writing. These comments can be recorded and may provide additional evidence upon which teachers can base their assessment.

Involving parents and other teachers

Parents, carers and other teachers who work with the children may offer a different perspective on the child as a writer from that of the child's class teacher. In particular, parents of bilingual children may be able to tell the teacher about the child's knowledge and understanding of writing in languages other than English. Similarly, parents or carers may talk to the teacher about their child's writing at home. Parents may talk about whether the child chooses to write, adds her own writing to letters written to relatives or friends, writes in a script other than English, is learning to write in another language at a Saturday school, or about the child's attitude towards writing. Information of this sort can help the teacher to understand the particular needs of all the children she teaches. The information will help to ensure that provision is being made within her planning for what they can do as well as for moving them towards the next level of attainment.

In addition to samples, observations, interactions and information from others, some teachers like to include checklists of development in writing in children's records. These sometimes take the form of a pre-printed list or wheel of common behaviours seen as children's writing develops. As the child reaches each stage of development itemized on the record, and once each stage occurs more than once in the child's writing, the relevant box is marked. In practice checklists are usually ticked or coloured in twice a term. A sample version of a checklist for writing development is reproduced in Figure 6.3.

Included in this are some of the stages that could be regarded as important landmarks in a child's development as a writer. Obviously these points could be changed or adapted to suit the needs of particular schools, classes, teachers and pupils.

Record-keeping as part of the school's assessment procedure can contribute to the enhancement of pupil learning and the professional development of teachers. At the start of a school year when one looks at a child's record one can see what the child's experiences as a learner have been to date. The record might include details such as attendance at nursery and languages that are spoken at home. The record will show the child's achievements and progress over the previous year. It will

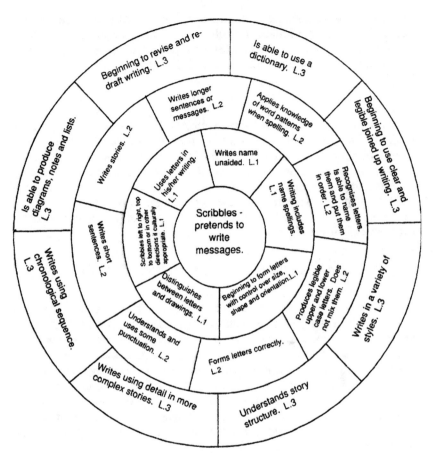

Figure 6.3

indicate what a child has covered previously and help the teacher to plan for the next stage of the child's learning. It will provide a starting point when thinking about how best to provide continuity and progression and help teachers to avoid repeating themes and topics that have already been covered.

As the school year continues, the collection of observations, interactions and samples that are added to the record at regular intervals will provide a helpful source book of information about the child's current learning, including the style and rate of learning. At the end of each term the progress of each child can be assessed and used to help with planning for the next term. The information contained in the record can be discussed with the child and with parents. Finally the record will be a source of evidence when making judgements about a child's progress as measured against the National Curriculum attainment targets. At the end of the school year the record can then be passed on to the child's next teacher who will continue the process.

Conclusion

Assessment is a critical element in the learning and teaching process. Over the past few years teachers have received a great deal of information about how and what to assess. This chapter has examined good practice in assessment and presented assessment as part of teaching and learning. If opportunities for assessment and record-keeping are built into the curriculum and classroom organization then they need not be seen as a burden but rather as a vital part of the learning process for both children and teachers.

Questions about assessment and record-keeping

Q. How do you assess style?

A. When looking at a collection of the child's writing one might expect to see the child using writing in many ways, including writing to produce stories, descriptions, accounts, records, letters, labels, notices and questions. Each of these types of writing has a particular form and so the teacher might expect to see the child using words in a way that is appropriate to the type of writing. In addition the teacher might look for detail, different ways of putting an obvious point, sequence, structure, clarity, use of simple and complex sentences, evidence of thought about how to interest the audience and consistent uses of tenses and pronouns in sentences and throughout a piece of writing.

Q. I like to make my own judgements about children. Why do I need to look at previous records?

A. Previous records indicate what things have been taught before and how they were taught. They show the types of writing the child has produced and whether a particular genre has been concentrated on. They show the progress the child has made, the child's strengths and weaknesses and the stage or level the child has reached as a writer. The previous teacher's comments about what the child needs to do next may be a useful starting point for the child's next teacher and the records can help teachers to avoid repetition in the writing curriculum. Each teacher will make her own judgements about children but previous records help to save time and present one perspective on the child as a learner.

7

Developmental Writing and the Bilingual Child

Introduction

This chapter contains two sections. The first section, 'Perceptions of bilingualism', examines how bilingualism is viewed in Britain and in school. The second section, 'Creating a learning environment for bilingual pupils', includes a number of practical suggestions for enabling bilingual pupils to become successful writers.

Perceptions of bilingualism

In many places throughout the world it is considered perfectly normal to be bilingual. Seventy per cent of the world's population operate as bilingual, often in countries which are usually known as monolingual. Many countries foster the acquisition of speaking, reading and writing in two or more languages and see bilingualism as an asset. However, despite being a multiracial and multicultural country where bilingual learners have been part of many school populations for a number of years, educationalists in Britain do not always seem to view bilingual learners positively and bilingual children are often described as a 'problem'. If, instead, this rich cultural diversity were valued and seen as a way of enriching our schools, colleges and universities, it could provide Britain with the possibility of becoming a bilingual or even a trilingual nation, but this is far from being the case.

In British classrooms many teachers and educationalists still encourage children to speak only in English even though this is not their first language. Teachers have been heard to say to pupils, 'Don't speak the language you speak at home here, you're in school now'. To other teachers they may say, 'The problem with this child's learning is her language, she's bilingual you know.' It is quite obvious from these comments that many teachers feel bilingualism equals problem equals failure. Savva (1990) states that, 'Bilingualism is a sensitive issue. It arouses strong emotions in teachers. They can feel defensive, threatened, guilty; they can feel that they are doing their best in difficult circumstances and with very little guidance or support.'

The problem seems to lie not necessarily in the children but in the way that bilingualism is viewed in Britain. Perceptions and anxieties seem to have been turned into educational 'theory' which students, teachers and educational planners have accepted. As a result many bilingual pupils have been isolated in classrooms, removed for 'special tuition', placed in special units for 'language delay' (Cummins, 1984) and continue to be disadvantaged by being tested on language ability through the medium of English at the age of seven. The standard assessment tasks (SATs) for speaking, listening, reading and writing can only be carried out in English although many children may be competent at speaking and listening, if not reading and writing, in languages other than English.

There seem to be two main reasons why bilingualism is seen as a problem in schools. The first is the way in which people are often judged by their use of language and the second is the effect of institutional racism on educationalists.

Language and the use of language are often used as general indicators of the status and position of the user. The more powerful a person is or the higher their status the more likely it is that their use of language will incorporate standard English and received pronunciation. Those who speak English with a dialect other than standard English and an accent other than received pronunciation are seen as less likely to hold power or to be in positions of high status. Although, intellectually, we are aware that non-standard dialects and non-received pronunciation do not equal low-status employment or intellectual inferiority, tradition still leads many of us to judge people by the way that they speak. If judgements about people are made on the way that they use language and if increasingly negative judgements are made about people as their use of language departs from standard English and received pronunciation, then many bilingual speakers and writers are likely to be judged harshly.

Racism is a sensitive area and provokes a great deal of discussion and some defensiveness in many teachers. However, racism is an integral part of the institutions that exist within British society and the education system is an institution that is subject to racist ideologies and practices just like any other institution (Epstein and Sealey, 1990). Racism operates at an unconscious and conscious level and affects all who live and work in Britain. It influences the way different groups of people, their culture and their language are viewed and in turn affects how bilingual learners are treated in school. If we are to begin to create a learning environment in which all children have the opportunity to succeed it is important to realize that racism does operate within the education system.

Changes in attitudes and practices are taking place. Research such as that by Dulay, Burt and Krashen (1982), which found that children who were actively encouraged to speak and write in their first language developed competency in a second language as quickly as their monolingual counterparts, has affected practice in schools. Practitioners have taken note of the suggestion that discouraging a child's first language can lead to language delay, difficulties in both languages and damage to self-esteem. Good educational practice which advocates accepting and valuing children as they are, recognizing their attributes and abilities and building upon and extending their learning from their own experience, coupled with an understanding of the issues surrounding bilingualism, has led to a number of local authorities, schools and teachers establishing exemplary practice with bilingual learners.

Creating a learning environment for bilingual pupils

If pupils are to succeed in their second language, it is essential that teachers create a classroom environment that is conducive to all pupils feeling that their heritage language and culture are valued and appreciated. An obvious way to do this is to reflect all the languages of all the pupils on the labels, captions and posters that are displayed around the school. Posters made by the teacher and the children might include one featuring the names of all the pupils in the class written in different scripts. The book corner and the books that children take home should contain languages other than English and have stories drawn from a variety of cultures. The listening area should contain tapes in a number of languages and story visuals should be made to accompany these tapes. This exposure to different languages benefits both bilingual and monolingual pupils. As Barrs *et al.* (1990) wrote,

> To help children to become successful users of English, the school curriculum needs to reflect the multicultural society, and to celebrate cultural and linguistic diversity. The bonus for the whole class will be what is learned from the awareness of language that bilingual children bring to the classroom – their bilingualism will lead the way in raising all children's awareness of language. This will give bilingual children continuing confidence in themselves as language users and learners.

This point is echoed in the non-statutory guidance for English (NCC, 1990, p. C2, para 2.10) which suggests that 'In implementing the programmes of study, different languages and different varieties of English should be valued and used in the classroom.'

Teachers and pupils can arrange play corners that reflect other cultures and ways of life, such as an Asian supermarket, a Chinese restaurant or a Turkish café. Artefacts and pictures that originate from the relevant cultures should be included within such areas and may include Asian spices and pulses, chopsticks, a wok and a Turkish teaset. Displays within the classroom and the school should include real objects and pictures that reflect the multicultural environment of the school and Britain today. Writing areas may contain writing implements from different cultures, such as Chinese paintbrushes, and alphabets in scripts other than English as well as dual-language dictionaries.

At school bilingual pupils do not need separating from their English-speaking peers; in fact this is totally counter-productive. It is essential that bilingual children feel part of the mainstream school, taking part in all its rituals, routines and classroom activities. Using and experiencing language in all its forms is the best way to learn and acquire it. When organizing the classroom for writing it is important to consider the nature of the activities that are planned. Teachers need to analyse the nature and organization of all language teaching for both bilingual and monolingual pupils in order to teach all pupils well. There should be opportunities for solitary, independent writing and also provision for collaborative activities where bilingual and monolingual pupils can work jointly together. The bilingual pupil will benefit greatly from working with a supportive partner who is speaking English in a setting that encourages real and meaningful communication. Similarly, the monolingual pupil may gain in her understanding of different languages and writing systems by working with a bilingual partner. Bilingual pupils' learning is enhanced by working on activities that contain real objects and that have a real outcome; examples of such activities include science experiments, model making and cooking. When the children are asked to write about what they have been doing and have found out, they will be able to draw upon the experiences they have shared together through the medium of a concrete activity.

Stories that originate from different traditions and histories should be told and may be used to promote writing. Teachers can tell these stories in English and then ask the pupils to create pictures to accompany the text. Bilingual writers can then follow the pictures and may produce writing in their own script. Simple puppets can be made by the pupils to accompany stories and texts, as can characters for magnet boards. Real visual clues help the bilingual speaker to make more sense of the story and text, particularly if they are accompanied by written captions which are familiar, such as story openings and endings including 'Once upon a time' or 'Once there lived a . . .' or 'And they all lived happily ever after'. Familiar and popular stories can be told and large books that retell the story can be produced by the pupils. It may be desirable to publish the book in all the languages that are spoken in the classroom. The pupil-made books can also be used as reading books that the children take home. Tapes in two or more languages can be recorded to accompany the books.

Teachers can provide collaborative talking, reading and writing activities for mixed groups of children. Games are often a successful way of involving all children in collaborative activities that encourage talk. There are a variety of language games that are particularly helpful in furthering bilingual pupils' language development, such as bingo games that have been specifically designed around favourite stories (Hester, 1983). These can be a good way of introducing pupils to oral and written forms of words. Base boards can be designed so that the story is told in words and pictures, words alone or pictures alone. As children become more proficient at reading and writing they can design their own games related to the stories with which they are familiar.

A bilingual teacher is a valuable resource who can usefully assist with the educational development of bilingual pupils, and some schools are lucky enough to have bilingual members of staff. Unfortunately there are not enough bilingual teachers in our schools so teachers may wish to ask parents and older brothers and sisters who are bilingual to assist with story telling and writing. If adults and older pupils see that their language and their culture are appreciated in the school they may be very willing to help out in the classroom. HMI (1990), discussing good practice in writing, suggested that collaboration between older and younger pupils at school is 'particularly valuable where the school is ethnically and culturally diverse'. It is essential that parents and friends are approached sensitively and their skills and contributions truly valued.

It is vital that teachers develop and extend their own knowledge about bilingualism so that they can positively encourage and aid the bilingual writer in all stages of her development. Teachers can quickly learn simple words and phrases that are commonly used within the classroom by bilingual children and can then include such words and phrases in stories or when addressing the class as a whole.

The Programme of Study for English suggests that children

whose parents are literate in a language other than English may have observed writing in their own first language, for which there may be a different writing system. Such awareness of writing in any form can help pupils to understand some of the functions of written language and should be used to promote their understanding of the functions of the English writing system.

(DES, 1990, p. 35)

Therefore it is essential that during the early stages of writing the bilingual child's first attempts are not dismissed, even if they are not legible to the teacher. The child needs to feel confident about her writing so that she will feel willing to write more and thus gain more knowledge and experience of print. For her knowledge of English to grow the child should not be discouraged from using her first language and the teacher should be alert to what bilingual learners bring to school in the way of knowledge about writing. Goodman wrote,

> Children who grow up with other forms of writing systems scribble differently, produce characters or letter like forms which resemble the orthographic system in their culture and write in the direction most conventional for their culture . . . Those who are not literate in . . . [that] . . . language may not . . . be able to read . . . [such writing] . . . but their forms are recognizable.

(Goodman, 1986, p. 10)

The role of the school is to extend the knowledge and understanding of writing that children bring to school. Therefore it is important to create an environment where children can have access to their first language. We need to value children's heritage languages and acknowledge children's full linguistic ability if all children are to have equal access to the curriculum. All children should be able to draw on the whole of their experience and knowledge about language in their education. For this reason it is useful to discuss the bilingual child's language and writing development with relatives and to establish whether the child is encouraged to write in her first language at home. Teachers need to find out as much as possible about the child's development and experiences so that they can provide writing activities in the classroom that best suit the child.

As was stated earlier in this book, children have to discover the uses and purposes of writing if they are to become competent and avid writers; therefore all children should be encouraged to write fluently and confidently in a range of situations. The writing development of bilingual pupils in their second language is very similar to that of monolingual pupils in their first language. Bilingual writers do not need tightly structured writing experiences that control their development, rather they need opportunities to write independently and with real purposes and for real audiences. 'Bilingual children should have opportunities to: use their existing language abilities and knowledge in different contexts, and for different and new purposes: [and] meet new language in contexts which are familiar'. (NCC, 1990).

The bilingual child's progress in writing will follow the stages of developmental writing outlined earlier in this book. There may be differences within each stage or some stages but these are not necessarily wrong, instead they may represent the child using her knowledge and experience of language systems other than English as she makes her early efforts at writing.

The samples of writing that follow represent the development of one bilingual pupil's writing during one school year in a Year 2 class. By September Sezgin had been in England for six months and had spent one term in the Year 1 class. Prior to coming to London he had attended school in Turkey. At first Sezgin was reluctant to write, his spoken English was developing slowly and he was unable to read alone in either Turkish or English; however, by about December of the Autumn term in the Year 2 class he was willing to write a great deal. He drew on his memory of words that had been introduced to the class through shared reading and class themes and incorporated these into all his writing. At this stage his writing was very difficult to read and, although Sezgin was willing to read his writing back, his difficulties with spoken English made it hard for the teacher to understand what Sezgin was trying to communicate. The teacher praised all Sezgin's efforts at writing and always commented on any words that she could read. This gave him greater confidence in his ability to write and he began to write long stories using his reading books as a source for spelling. The example in Figure 7.1 shows a story he wrote about a visit to a friend's house in February. It is very difficult to read but shows how Sezgin found words around the classroom to incorporate into his writing. He was experimenting with some spellings on his own, such as HES for *his* and WES for *was*. At this stage he was mainly using capital letters in his writing.

The example of Sezgin's writing shown in Figure 7.2 was written in June. The children were writing their own reports. These were to be put in a booklet that they were making and were to accompany the end-of-year reports that the teacher would send home. This extract contains Sezgin's feelings about his learning in mathematics and English. This was a first draft. Sezgin was very clear about the task and communicates very effectively. Most of his spelling is correct and again he referred to books to find the correct spellings of many words. The writing reflects how Sezgin used his spoken English to help him construct his sentences: he omits some words such as *and* and *at* and inserts others such as *a*. For words that he found very difficult to write, such as *addition* and *division*, he has used the mathematical notation but the meaning is clear. Sezgin was aware that the main purpose of writing was to communicate.

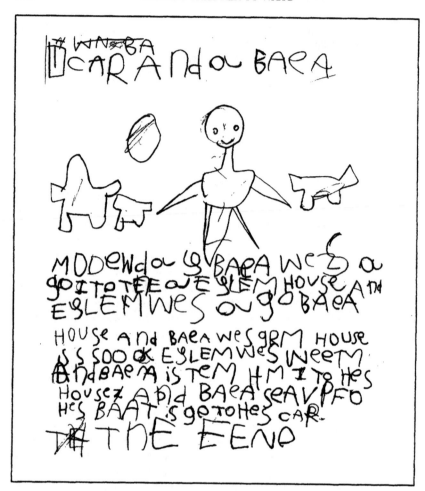

Figure 7.1

Sezgin went through many of the stages of development that were described earlier in this book. The teacher was able to intervene throughout his writing career with encouragement and models and suggest the next step for this child so that he would make progress as a writer. By the age of seven he was well on the way to becoming a competent writer.

Despite variations in background and writing systems, the bilingual child is able to succeed in school in much the same way as the monolingual child does when teachers are committed to meeting the needs of all our children in a truly child-centred environment. For this reason the bilingual child's language and culture must be appreciated by the staff

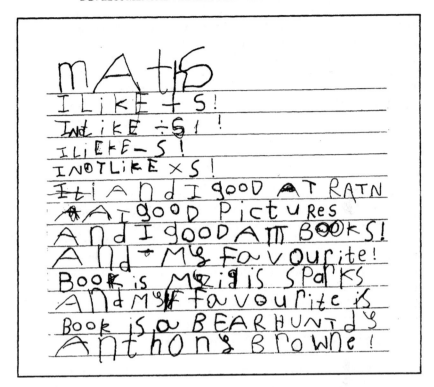

Figure 7.2

within the school, the pupils and the community, and the child should be integrated fully into the life of the school. Bilingual children have the right to have their needs catered for so that they have access to a rich and comprehensive curriculum. To provide real equality of opportunity for all pupils, we as teachers must meet the challenge of creating a learning environment that recognizes differences amongst pupils and accepts and values all cultures. To this end, schools and teachers need to demonstrate that cultural diversity enriches school environments and extends the learning of all pupils.

Conclusion

Bilingual pupils are present in many schools in Britain today. They come to school with knowledge and experiences that are different from their monolingual counterparts. These differences are not detrimental to their learning as long as schools and teachers create a learning environment that celebrates cultural diversity and provides opportunities for full participation by bilingual pupils. Learning in a first language must be acknowledged and allowed to develop alongside the learning of English, so that pupils bring what they know about being a language user to the learning of a new language. The teacher should support bilingual writers by providing them with a range of writing activities, real reasons for writing and praise and encouragement for all their efforts and successes.

Questions about writing and bilingual pupils

Q. I have an Urdu pupil in my class; she is reluctant to write, what can I do?

A. First of all consider how she feels about her language, does she see it represented within the school, does she hear her language spoken within the classroom? Are her language and culture being positively reinforced? Depending upon which stage of English the child is at she will need time to adapt to the ways of the school and the classroom. The child should be encouraged to work as a group member on tasks that require her full involvement. The pupil should also be encouraged to 'have a go' at writing in situations within which she can experiment and be allowed to make mistakes with language.

Q. I have never taught bilingual pupils before: what would be my starting point for writing?

A. Bilingual pupils should be expected to write in the same way as the monolingual members of the class. The teacher may clarify the task by providing additional explanations and demonstrations, or by asking them to work with more confident partners, but the starting point and expectation should be the same for all children. As soon as they produce a written response to an activity the teacher can use this to analyse what the child knows, provide encouragement to write more and demonstrate more information about writing.

8

The Hidden Curriculum of Writing

Introduction

This chapter examines the hidden curriculum of writing with regard to gender. It looks at how the writing of boys and girls differs in content and presentation and considers ways in which the organization of writing affects what and how boys and girls write. Within each section there are suggestions of practical steps that teachers may take when planning a writing curriculum that gives boys and girls the opportunity to achieve their potential as well-rounded writers.

Gender and writing

The area of language and literacy may seem to many to be a neutral part of the curriculum. Teachers often believe that their role is simply to teach children to read and write and that this teaching is not influenced by prejudices, commonly held ideas, misconceptions or stereotypes. However, there is a growing body of evidence about the relationship between language, literacy and gender which suggests that, despite changes in the nature and organization of the curriculum, the language learning process is strongly gender differentiated and girls and boys do learn to be literate in different ways (Spender and Spender, 1980; Swann and Graddol, 1988; Whitehead, 1990). White wrote,

> If teachers are to counter the gendered outcomes of schooling they need to be prepared to intervene in the literacy development of pupils with a clear explicit knowledge of the way language works at all levels of meaning creation. The generic structures of speech and writing shape and create the knowledge of schools subjects, but they simultaneously shape the identities of speakers and writers. Without a knowledge of how meanings are made through language, teachers

are liable to unconscious collusion in the repetition of sex-stereo-typed educational practices.

(White, 1990 p. 182)

How are gendered outcomes demonstrated in the writing that young children produce? If one compares and analyses the writing produced by boys and girls in response to the same task one can often see clear gender differentiation in content and style. To illustrate this point, four stories, two written by girls and two written by boys, are reproduced below. The children are all aged seven. The first two stories, both entitled 'The Spooky House', were written when the children were working on the theme of homes. The children drafted and redrafted their stories over the period of a week.

'The Spooky House' by Samantha

Once upon a time there was a spooky house. In the spooky house there lived a witch who had a pink cat. She wanted to catch children to help her in her spooky house. There was a ghost there too and he was called Boo Hoo. One day the witch went out to the woods and saw a little girl with long hair. She thought she was lovely and wanted to catch her, so she put a net over her head and told her she was going to the spooky house. The little girl cried and the witch let her go. The ghost and the witch then made friends with the girl and they went back to the spooky house for tea. They all lived happily ever after.

'The Spooky House' by Aaron

Once there was a spooky house and a vampire lived there. He had blood in his lips and hair in his ears. He had a big black coat and sharp claws. He liked eating dead children but he had run out of dead children so he needed to catch some. He went into the forest and saw a little boy and girl having a picnic. He thought, 'Hurrah, I will kill them and eat them.' He hid behind a tree and then jumped on them. The little girl cried and the little boy cried. The vampire got out his sharp claws and killed them. His lips had blood all over them. He took them back to the spooky house and kept them there dead.

Samantha's story concentrates on emotions. It tells of loneliness, reconciliation and friendship and ends happily for all three characters. In contrast, Aaron's story is bloodthirsty and violent. It shows the powerful preying on the weak and concludes with the success of the aggressor.

The next stories were written as illustrated story-books to be shared with children in the reception class. One of the teacher's aims when introducing this task was to encourage the children to produce anti-sexist stories. She discussed the project with the children in depth and commented on the children's suggestions with particular reference to gender. In spite of her intervention many of the stories that resulted again reflected gendered outcomes.

'The Shopping Basket' by Jane

One day a mum said to Steven, 'Pop down to the shops for me please.' Steven buys six eggs and five packets of crisps and some flowers to stand in the hall. He went off carrying his Mum's basket and arrived at home. When he went back to the shop a pig said, 'Give me one of those eggs.' Steven said, 'If I throw a egg up in the air you are so clumsy I bet you could not catch it.' When he came to the litter basket there was a goat. 'Give me a packet of crisps or I will butt you up the bum.' The goat said that Steven was stupid. His Mum said, 'Where have you been all this time?' His Mum said, 'Come on have your tea now.' She put an egg on the table. Steven said, 'I met some animals on the way to the shops.' His Mum said, 'Eat your tea.'

'The Car Lesson' by Glen

One day a boy called Andrew wanted a car and his Dad said, 'No you are too young and you can't afford it.' The boy said, 'But you can let me work in the pub and pay me.' His Dad had a TRANSAN car and it was red and shining. He took Andrew for a lesson in it and he went to Snetterton and tested the car and he went CRAZY all over the circuit. He got stuck in the gravel pit 200 hundred times and then went home. He passed his driving lesson and had a party in the pub. He had a pint of beer and then went home.

Jane's story has met the aim of catering for a younger audience and is based on the book *The Shopping Basket* (Burningham, 1980). She has chosen a subject that is within her experience and familiar to her. The story finishes with mum cooking the tea and concludes with the sentence, 'Eat your tea', a statement familiar to all good mums. In contrast, Glen's story is much more action packed. The story is full of technical language and even ends stereotypically with the male hero 'going to the pub' to finish off his eventful day. How many stories, books or plays end with the main female character going to the pub for a pint? Very few, one would guess!

These four stories are typical examples of children's writing and reveal quite distinct differences between how and what boys and girls write. Imaginative writing by children requires close scrutiny to identify the particular biases and influences that they are subject to and incorporate into their lives. If the writing children do at school is not just to become another avenue for girls and boys to rehearse and reproduce what they have already learned about the roles and experiences of males and females in society, the writing that children are asked to do needs careful consideration. Children's choices need to be analysed with the pupils, and gender issues must be raised in order to provide alternative perspectives to the institutional influences that are part of pupils' lives. The sorts of interventions teachers make need to be systematic, powerful, constant and reinforced by personal belief and understanding. Providing the occasional story starter that includes a central girl character is not in any way adequate since this is not sufficient to challenge the controlling mechanisms that exist within the arena of language and gender.

Starting points for writing

Recently a Year 2 teacher was discussing possible titles for class books with the children. The class contained fairly equal numbers of boys and girls. The children were all sitting in the book area of the classroom and the teacher was noting down the children's suggestions on a flip chart. He began the discussion by asking the children what their favourite television programmes were. A host of hands went up, mainly those of the boys. They suggested *Turtles, Thundercats, Batman,* etc. The teacher praised the children for so many suggestions and told them that these would be good starting points for their own stories. The group, mainly boys, that had volunteered the answers began to shout 'yeah' and raise their fists into the air. The teacher quietened the class down and then asked one girl what she would like to write about. The child did not answer and was questioned further by the teacher. Eventually she said, 'Blue Peter'. The class burst into laughter and one boy told her that *Blue Peter* was not a story and that it was boring. The girl said nothing. The teacher told the girl that *Blue Peter* might be a difficult starting point for a story and invited her to think again. The girl declined.

This example shows how one teacher attempted to stimulate his class into writing imaginatively. He believed that by beginning the class discussion with a mention of television programmes he would hold his pupils' attention and motivate them into wanting to write. The teacher succeeded in catching the attention of many of the children but the topics that were identified and the behaviour of some of the pupils excluded many other children. The teacher's choice of television programmes for beginning this work was at the very best misguided and at worst tantamount to reinforcing numerous gender and racial stereotypes. He had not considered the way that boys, girls, men and women are represented on television. When the teacher was met with shouts about *Batman* and *Thundercats* he simply saw this as a discipline problem, not as an assertion of the boys' power and aggression. The teacher attempted to include the girl within the discussion but his attempts led to her feeling isolated and threatened, hence her silence and refusal to answer any more questions. The teacher did not deal with the boys' response to *Blue Peter* but allowed the boys to intimidate the girl with their comments, therefore isolating her even more. The example above was not a deliberate attempt by the teacher to be nasty or to differentiate between pupils according to gender; his intentions were good. As he wanted to identify a stimulating starting point for writing he began with something that is familiar to most children. However, he had not thought out his starting point and even when many of the class were alienated by the discussion he did not rethink his strategies or even stop the discussion.

This example shows how and why teachers need to be aware of the content they select and the way in which they interact with pupils in the classroom. If teachers praise certain ideas and behaviour, they are 'telling' the class what they feel to be good, commendable, exciting, important and so on. Similarly, if teachers ignore or avoid particular issues that arise they may be silently reinforcing what the pupils already know.

Before beginning to plan the writing curriculum it is important to consider the scope of the theme that is selected and to avoid choosing themes that are obviously gender biased. Will it enable the teacher to present a balanced view of boys and girls, and men and women? A theme such as 'Conquerers and invaders' is likely to have limitations for most classroom practitioners, whereas themes such as 'Change, patterns' or 'Ourselves and our society' provide many more opportunities to explore issues of gender. When considering the types of writing that can emerge from the theme the teacher should try to create a balance between imaginative, personal and factual types of writing. She should ensure that girls have equal access to factual writing such as writing up experiments and that boys have the opportunity for personal writing. Keeping a diary is one way of promoting reflection and thoughtfulness. Personal diaries should be regarded as the private property of the individual pupil and, unless the pupil in question chooses to show her writing to someone, it should not be read by anyone, not even the teacher. With reference to imaginative writing the teacher needs to select starting points that challenge gender stereotypes. The teacher needs to monitor what is being written and how it is being written. The children should be questioned about their choice of content and challenged if the writing reflects stereotypical and prejudiced ideas. The choice of particular titles for writing should reflect the experiences of all the children in the class. The teacher may decide to use positive discrimination when setting writing tasks. Boys may be asked to write a story that requires the central male character to be gentle and thoughtful while girls could write a science fiction adventure. If children are asked to retell a familiar story the teacher should make sure that all the messages in the story are considered and the children are given time to reflect and comment about them. For example, discussions about *Little Red Hiding Hood* often ignore the intelligence and wit that Red Riding Hood displays, focusing instead on the strong and intimidating presence of the wolf. Discussions of this story could examine why it features a girl and how she manages to outwit the wolf and protect herself. Before the children write, the teacher needs to provide equal time for both girls and boys to discuss their ideas. She should try to ensure that the boys listen to the girls and value their ideas. Finally, as children write, the teacher needs to assess how as well as what they write. Do boys write more if the writing is factual or technical? Are girls more inclined to write a longer piece of writing if the story is an imaginative one? Teachers need positively to encourage both boys and girls to write to the best of their ability across a range of types of writing if all children are to achieve their potential as writers.

Teacher expectation

The Thomas Report (ILEA, 1985) emphasized the important effect that teacher expectation has on pupil achievement. Quite simply, pupils achieve more if teachers hold higher expectations of them, provide opportunities for children to achieve their best, and focus upon the process of learning as well as the product. We would all want to adhere to the principle of wanting the best for the children we teach; however, teachers do hold particular views relating to gender that may impinge upon pupil success and may prevent some children from experiencing a broad and differentiated writing curriculum.

Research has indicated that boys and girls hold very different attitudes towards writing. Girls often favour writing activities, particularly imaginative work and poetry, while boys feel less competent at writing and prefer factual and technical writing to more personal types of writing. These views are not genetic; they are created by the institutional and societal examples that children see around them (Swann, 1992).

The infant school has often been described as a 'feminine' environment where female role models heavily outnumber males and where traditional female qualities such as quietness, care and passivity are fostered. Writing and reading are often viewed as feminine activities that appeal more to girls than to boys since they require quietness and passivity. Many people do not value success in English as highly as success in science or mathematics since it can be perceived as lacking the usefulness of subjects that can lead to entry into male-dominated, technical professions. One often hears adults say that boys are better at mathematics and girls are better at English. These attitudes affect children and may contribute to the way that boys and girls approach writing. They may limit boys' performance in writing and persuade girls that reading and writing are girls' activities, rather than curriculum areas that should be valued and worked on by all pupils.

Girls are often expected to be better at all aspects of writing, including handwriting and presentation. Many teachers still equate neat handwriting and length with girls' writing and exciting content and untidy handwriting with boys' writing. When children are planning and drafting their work, teachers often expect the boys to spend far less time in perfecting their work, while girls are expected to pay more attention to detail and take a greater length of time to complete the first draft before producing the final copy.

When children are asked to read their writing aloud, either to the class or for an assembly, boys are often chosen to read because they have louder voices. As we all know, this is not necessarily the case; however, teachers often feel that boys are 'louder' and reinforce this stereotype by selecting boys and omitting girls from this activity. All children should be encouraged to share their writing with an audience. If children do this by reading aloud, the quieter reader will need praise and encouragement and the rest of the children will need to be reminded to listen to others with patience and consideration.

Changing one's views and beliefs takes time and consideration. It involves finding out more about how beliefs were formed, reflecting upon these beliefs and making gradual, yet sustained changes when working within the classroom and the school. In order to give all children the opportunity to succeed at writing it is important to review one's own expectations and practices in relation to boys and girls and literacy. We need to ask ourselves how the boys approach the writing curriculum? Do boys spend less time on writing and do they consider it to be less important than other subjects? Given a particular writing activity do they rush the work and give less attention to style and detail? Are girls spending more time writing and concentrating more on handwriting and presentation? Do girls spend more time writing creative and imaginative pieces rather than technical or scientific scripts? If the answer to these questions is 'Yes' then it is important to try to emphasize to all pupils that writing is an important part of the curriculum and that high standards are expected from all the children. Boys will need to be encouraged to work on more personal and emotional pieces of writing and girls to write more factually and technically. The teacher will need to praise the boys for well-presented writing and encourage girls to take a chance with their ideas rather than allowing them to spend a long time on presenting a perfect copy.

Organization of the writing curriculum

When children are writing at school they need access to writing tools and resources and the space and atmosphere to be able to write competently. We all seek to create this atmosphere by providing the necessary equipment and space. However, the organization for writing does also depend upon other factors. Firstly, how are groups formed and structured for discussion, collaboration and response? Do girls and boys behave differently in these situations? Do they offer and accept different kinds of support and response? Recently a class of Year 1 children were observed discussing the care of babies as part of the their class theme 'Ourselves'. A parent had come into school to bath her new baby and both boys and girls were excited by this event. The teacher was particularly concerned with gender stereotyping and had organized the class so that all the children could have an equal say in the discussion. During the discussion the teacher put equal numbers of questions to the boys and the girls. She was careful to ask boys questions that involved thinking about the care of babies and girls about the more technical aspects of child care that involved thinking about water temperature and suitable clothing. As the discussion continued, one boy put his hand up and said he was fed up with letting everybody talk when he knew all the answers, and he continued to complain that it was not fair that everybody had to have a turn at answering when they didn't know what they were talking about. The teacher responded to this child by asking the rest of the class what they thought about his opinion. They told him that it was fair that everyone had a turn to speak. Later, when the children were asked to write about the discussion the teacher made sure that the boy who had expressed his personal discontent worked with a group of children who sat with her. She made sure that each child's view could be expressed in that group's contribution to the class book. This example demonstrates careful and sensitive teacher intervention and rigorous planning and structuring of the oral discussion and organization for writing.

In order that every child can make a contribution to discussions and writing it is necessary for the teacher to encourage the art of collaboration, to make sure that girls are listened to, to make sure that boys participate in groups without dominating, and to organize sessions so that boys and girls have equal turns at leading discussions and taking notes of the discussion. The teacher may have to remind the boys that they have to listen and scribe while girls lead the discussion or activity. At times it may be necessary to have all-boy groups and all-girl groups and to structure the writing that each group does so that each group can respond differently to the task. For example, if the children are working on a class or group story the teacher may organize the writing so that girls take the lead in writing the more powerful and controlling parts of the story and the boys are responsible for the more passive and emotional parts of the story. When children are using the word processor the teacher may need to ensure that girls have as much time using the computer as the boys and that both boys and girls have turns at composing as well as controlling the keyboard. Collaborative working is hard to achieve, therefore teachers will have to be ready to intervene to balance the contribution made by boys and girls.

Resources

Children are directly influenced by what they see around them and by what they read and their understanding of society is reflected and reinforced in their writing. Therefore pupils need to witness resources that portray female and male roles positively and in a way that challenges stereotypes. Pictures, posters, displays and books should reflect a variety of experiences and depict the roles of men and women in non-stereotypical ways. Teachers will need to consider their resources carefully, by reading the books that are in their classrooms and removing sexist material, by purchasing resources that reflect the world in the twentieth century, and by displaying children's work that complements an anti-sexist approach to education.

Conclusion

Creating a learning environment that takes proper account of the needs of boys and girls takes time, educational support, finance, excellent resources, and realistic and balanced teacher expectations. It cannot be created in haste and will not function correctly if tokenistic strategies are employed. Schools need to consider their curriculum, expectations, organizational structures and resources carefully and thoughtfully in order to make equal opportunities for all a reality rather than a dream. The intention of this chapter is to provide teachers with a starting point for discussion and with ideas for creating such a reality.

Questions about the hidden curriculum and writing

Q. Girls tend to do better at writing than boys so why do I need positive discrimination in favour of the girls when organizing for writing?
A. Language can be a means of reinforcing stereotypical representations and limiting choices. If we are interested in equal opportunities then it is important to recognize that the writing curriculum can help to transmit values that may limit the experiences of all children. Therefore it is important that all children engage in a range of writing activities that enables them to explore as many aspects of being human as possible.

Q. How do I stop boys from writing about aggressive and stereotypical topics?

A.   To do this the teacher will, at times, have to give boys set topics to write about, organize the children to work in mixed collaborative pairs and intervene in boys' writing at the planning and drafting stage. She will need to make awareness of the hidden curriculum of writing part of her classroom writing programme.

9

Parents and Writing

Introduction

This chapter looks at the contribution parents make to their children's writing development before they start school and the ways in which parents can become involved in helping children to write after they start school. It suggests some strategies for schools to use when explaining developmental writing to parents and other interested adults.

Writing before school

Before children start school most of them will be aware of writing. Most children grow up in an environment where they are surrounded by print, from teletext to the writing on packaging. Many children will have had experience of books and stories being read to them and many children will have seen adults at home writing shopping lists and notes and filling in forms. From these experiences children have some understanding of how the writing system works. This early awareness of print is well documented in the writing of Bissex (1980), Ferreiro and Teberosky (1979) and Goodman (1986). The Programme of Study for writing (DES, 1990) acknowledges that 'Pupils will have seen different kinds of writing in the home – their names on birthday cards or letters, forms, shopping lists and so on.'

Many children begin to make their first attempts at writing before they begin school. They imitate the role models that adults and older children present to them and the writing that they see in books and their environment. They may identify their pictures and possessions with early attempts at their own name. Children may also have had experiences of writing in collaboration with adults at home. They may have signed greeting cards and added their own writing to letters written by adults. Parents may have shown children how to write their name and given children notebooks, pens, pencils and workbooks to encourage them to write. Children who have attended a nursery or a playgroup may have had additional opportunities to experiment with writing. All this experience and understanding of writing that children bring to school should not be disregarded by teachers. School is the place where writing continues rather than where it begins and the teacher's role is to appreciate and extend the understanding and opportunities for writing that children have. As children's experience of print through books and reading increases and as teachers make the features of the English writing system explicit, children's writing will develop in range and legibility.

When parents enroll their child for school and bring the child to school for her pre-entry visits, teachers can discuss with them the child's early experiences of literacy. This provides teachers with important information about the child and signals to parents the important contribution that they can make to their child's learning. Parents' comments about their child's writing at home will help teachers to know what children can already do and what experiences they have had and will help them to plan effectively to extend each child's achievement in writing.

Explaining developmental writing to parents

Many parents will have memories of learning to write at school. They will probably remember writing their news, using a rubber and learning spellings for spelling tests. They may also remember the sorts of comments that teachers wrote on their writing, such as 'sp' or 'very untidy' or 'very neat work'. They may still feel self-conscious as writers because they think that their spelling is not very good. Many parents will probably have been the recipients of a message from school that writing is about accurate and neat presentation rather than the communication of a message. This view of writing is reinforced by the press and the media when they report on the supposed falling standards in literacy. Parents' understanding of the writing process and their expectations about how children will learn at school may often reflect their own school experiences. The way that writing is now taught in school will probably be very different from parents' memories so it is important to explain how it differs and why schools endorse particular approaches to the teaching of writing.

Change is often difficult for people to accept, particularly if they do not understand the reasons for the change. One hears people (teachers as well as parents) say such things as, 'In my day we did it this way and it never did me any harm' or 'We had spelling tests and I learned to write.' This may be the case. However, change usually takes place because discoveries have led to better ways of doing things. Forty years ago there were very few washing machines or refrigerators in people's homes, now most people regard these as essential and people have benefited from the convenience of having them. The aim of research and new knowledge is to lead to developments that improve conditions for people. In schools teachers implement change to make learning easier for the pupils and more relevant to their needs as adults of the twenty-first century. When writing, children no longer need to be able to produce perfectly formed copperplate script in order to take up a career as a clerk as was the case at the beginning of this century. Now secretaries use word processors with spreadsheet and database facilities and their personal handwriting style is often only important to themselves. It is even possible to use a personal computer to fill in application forms.

Change in educational practice takes place for two reasons: to improve learning and to accommodate new understanding. These reasons can be explained to parents in the following ways.

Firstly, things were not always wonderful in the 'good old days'. Many children left school unable to write competently and confidently. Figures 9.1 and 9.2 are extracts from two letters that I have received recently that show the sorts of errors that adults make when they are writing. These examples indicate that the more formal methods of the 1950s and 1970s when these writers went to school did not necessarily succeed with all pupils.

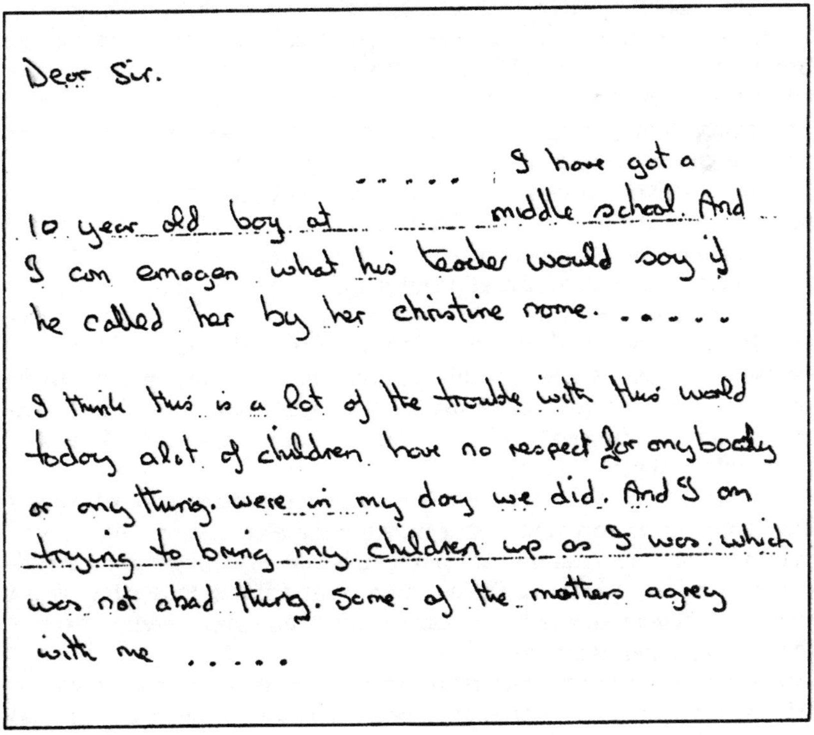

Dear Sir.

..... I have got a 10 year old boy at ..... middle school. And I can emogen what his teacher would say if he called her by her christine name. .....

I think this is a lot of the trouble with this world today alot of children have no respect for anybody or anything. were in my day we did. And I am trying to bring my children up as I was. which was not abad thing. Some of the mothers agrey with me .....

Figure 9.1

22.4.1992

Miss Browne

Dear Doctor,
The above patient recived chiropody treatment from on the above date,she
had a very painful nail Ist onleft foot the nail was deeply enbedded in the
nail groove as the nail looked like a onychophosis nail ,I enqiured if there is
is any more of her family got nails like this to which I wasinformed it was
passed down from her father.
    As you will see the nail is thickas well, I thought she should see you
as I think in some one of this age a peice of nail and root could be removed
, not all but were it bend in.
    I consider it would be worth doing to save a lot of pain in the future.

Yours Sincerely

Figure 9.2

In the past many children left school unwilling to write. Because writing is an integral part of school life in terms of homework, note-making and writing examination answers, many children lost out in all aspects of education because of their poor attitude towards writing. By changing the approach to writing in school, teachers are hoping to promote competence and confidence. A developmental approach to writing seems to foster a positive approach to writing in young children, and educationalists hope that this desire to write will stay with children throughout their school career and beyond.

Secondly, the level of educationalists' understanding about learning in general and learning to write has improved. This search for better teaching that helps rather than hinders learning is at the heart of teachers' professionalism. Teachers want children to learn and to succeed at school and this is why they change approaches, resources and the curriculum. At all times teachers are seeking to act in the best interests of children's achievement.

Parents more readily believe what teachers say when they know and trust them. This process may take time but if the children are happy and successful at school parents can not dismiss the evidence that their children are making progress. The enthusiasm of children for writing when they write developmentally can not be ignored and may convince parents that teachers are teaching well.

The next step may be to explain to parents how this approach works. All the staff of the school should be familiar with the approach and committed to working in a developmental way so that they can answer questions from parents, carers, governors and inspectors. The school's policy on developmental writing should be outlined in the school prospectus, be available as a writing policy and be explained to parents at English curriculum evenings. From time to time it might be possible to present children's writing in the form of a display for parents. This could show how one individual's writing has changed over time or it could feature samples from different children showing how writing develops as children get older and become more experienced at writing. It might be helpful for teachers to include the relevant attainment targets and quotations from the Programme of Study for English that are illustrated by the writing on display to demonstrate to parents that the school's methods for teaching writing have the support of the National Curriculum recommendations.

One way of explaining to parents and governors about the approach to writing that is used in the school is to organize a curriculum evening to which all interested adults are invited. There are many reasons for holding a curriculum evening. The staff may decide to hold one before introducing developmental writing, to give information about the approach currently in use at school, or when seeking volunteers to help with writing in school. Even if developmental writing is already in place in the school and most parents seem to be aware of this and supportive of the approach, there may be a group of parents who are new to the school and who do not understand the way that writing is taught. If developmental writing is an established part of the curriculum, schools may choose to hold a literacy evening where the focus is on maintaining parental interest in helping children with writing and reading at home. Whatever the reason the aim is always the same. It is to answer questions and give information so that adults can support children's learning at school and at home.

Even though the intention is to provide explanations, it is more interesting if the evening is arranged as a series of workshop sessions in which adults participate. Workshops encourage adults to discuss new insights and problems with each other and with the teachers. Personal understanding is often gained by becoming actively involved rather than by just listening.

Below is a list of suggestions for activities that could be included in a writing curriculum evening. Schools might like to select activities from this list that would be most appropriate for their purposes.

Welcome and introduction
The focus of this would be to explain the purpose and format of the evening to all who have attended.

How and why do we write?

Ask the adults, in pairs, to make a list of all the writing they can remember doing during the previous seven days. When the lists are complete ask how people wrote some of the things on their lists. If, for example, someone has written a note to the milk deliverer you might ask, 'What was it written on? How long did it take to write? What was it written with?' If someone has written a formal letter they could be asked, 'What was it written on? How long did it take to write? Was it written out more than once? If so, what was corrected on the second draft and how was it corrected? What was it written with?'

The answers to these questions should produce some interesting points about the factors that affect how we write and the reasons for writing. At this point, audience, purpose, style, transcription, composition and any other issues that emerge from the lists that the parents have generated can be discussed.

Teachers can compare the range of writing that has been identified by the adults with the variety of opportunities for writing that are offered to children at school. It might be helpful to refer to the Programme of Study for writing, spelling and handwriting that details the different types of writing that children are expected to engage in at school.

The writing process

Talk to the adults about the process of writing. Use overheads of the children's writing to show how development occurs over time and to explain how writing is learnt. Discuss how and when teachers intervene and correct children's writing.

Spelling

Give the parents a spelling test of ten commonly misspelt words. This should illustrate the point that spelling is a difficult skill for most people. The teachers can then explain that spelling needs teaching in a systematic way. The teachers might explain the 'look, cover, remember, write, check' approach that is used in school. This could be illustrated by 'teaching' the adults how to spell one of the words from the spelling test using this method.

Handwriting

Ask the adults to look at all the writing they have done so far during the evening and to consider whether it was uniformly neat, well formed and legible. Was there any crossing out in the spelling test? Did the neatness matter? If someone else was reading the writing would they copy it out? When does handwriting matter? Follow this by discussing the school's policy on handwriting.

Adults writing
The parents can be asked to write a short description of the evening that can be read by the children the next day. They should be given a time limit. Observe how the adults approach and carry out the task. Give feedback on what writers do when they write. Issues such as drafting, making mistakes, presentation, audience, and the need to spend time on writing should arise from this activity.

Writing a book
If children have been invited to the session, ask parents and children to work together to write a book. The parents could write a story drawn from their memories of their own childhood. The children could illustrate the book. Again the adults should see that writing is not straightforward. It calls for planning and drafting and it takes time to produce something for someone to read. The adults might like to continue and complete this activity at home.

Helping at home
Give parents some ideas about how they can help with writing at home in ways that will support the school's approach to writing.

Helping at school
Explain and give examples of how adults can help with writing at school. Ask for volunteers.

Displays
As a backdrop to the whole evening have displays of children's writing and the books that they have made arranged around the school. Display first drafts as well as the final piece of writing. Provide written explanations of the work and, if appropriate, link the writing that is displayed to the National Curriculum Programmes of Study and statements of attainment.

Questions
Answer questions fairly and honestly. If teachers can convince parents of their interest in children's progress it is likely that the parents will support the approach advocated by the school.

Hopefully, by the end of the evening all the adults present will have remembered how hard writing can be, that it is rarely right first time, that sometimes ideas are hard to find, and that neatness is not necessarily the most important part of writing. They may have gained some insights into the way that the staff of the school attempt to make writing easier and more purposeful for the pupils whilst helping the children to succeed at writing.

How parents can help with writing at school

For many years parental involvement in education has been viewed as a means of enhancing children's development and learning at school. Recently the Education Reform Act (1988) has defined the central role that parents have in the education of their children in two ways. First, parents are acknowledged to have an important part to play in the education of their children before and outside school and, second, parents have to be informed of their children's progress at school through the framework of the National Curriculum and its associated assessments so that they can support their child's learning at home and at school (HM Government, 1988).

Most teachers have welcomed parental involvement in school and have acknowledged the contribution that adults can make in the classroom. Often parents have assisted teachers by sharing their skills and experiences with groups of children and by listening to children read. In addition to hearing reading there are a great many ways in which parents, relatives and friends can use their oral and written language abilities in the classroom to extend and enhance the literacy curriculum and more specifically the writing curriculum at school.

Many parents and carers have experience of sharing stories with children at home. Those who are confident may read or tell stories to groups of children at school. Less confident adults may choose to record stories on tape for children to listen to in the listening corner. Both these activities are particularly valuable for bilingual pupils if the adults concerned can share stories in community languages. Sometimes adults can be asked to write books for children. These may be stories, as in the project described by Clover and Gilbert (1984), or they may be descriptions of their own childhood. The latter may become a useful resource for history or geography teaching in school as well as being a way for children to see authors other than themselves at work. Many adults have little experience of writing in this way after they leave school and they can find this activity difficult. This may be a good reminder to parents about how difficult writing can be for young children and may provide them with insights into the value of drafting and collaboration. Recipes can be written out by parents who may then come into school to help the children cook the dish that was described. As well as sharing and producing writing, adults can work with children who are writing. They can act as scribes for the children, type their stories on to the word processor for them as they compose, discuss ideas and listen to children reading their own stories.

Bilingual parents can provide the school with translations of signs and notices that can be displayed with writing in English. They can be asked to translate the children's own stories from English to the language of the home or vice versa. They may also provide translations for popular reading books that are used in the classroom. Adults can provide writing or write in the classroom in a number of ways. All the writing that they do is an excellent lesson for children who will see that writing is a valuable skill in which adults engage.

How parents can help with writing at home

An acceptance of developmental learning means that learning does not only begin when children start school, nor does learning end when children leave school each day. Learning and experimenting with learning take place both inside and outside school. Thus it is important for teachers to value what children can do when they begin school and to acknowledge the importance of learning beyond school. With a developmental approach to writing, children are defined as writers from the time when they begin to make marks on paper that represent words and ideas. These early attempts at writing usually begin at home.

Hall (1987) argues that children's early writing produced before school is not always perceived as writing by parents. They do not recognize early scribble as the precursor to later writing. If little value is given to early attempts to write then opportunities for practising writing may be restricted to adult-controlled contexts such as children writing their names on greeting cards. Czerniewska (1992) suggests that when parents are encouraged to value their children's early writing they gain a new perspective on writing. Thus it is important that teachers and workers in nurseries and playgroups are aware of the significance of children's early marks on paper so that they can explain this to parents. If children's early writing is valued and praised, children are likely to be encouraged to do more and so increase their knowledge, understanding and skills associated with writing. Disseminating information to parents of children who are already at school may affect the way that adults view the writing produced by younger sisters and brothers and help parents understand the beginnings of writing.

In 1989 a report was published containing the results of a survey of parental help given with writing to children at home (Hall et al., 1989). This survey found that 85 per cent of the 426 parent respondents did help their children with writing at home. Parents do provide help with spelling and handwriting and often buy workbooks for their children to practise copying letters and words. There is usually an enormous amount of interest from adults in a child's progress in writing once she begins school. If parents are not guided by the school in the sort of help that they can easily provide they will continue to instruct children in the transcription elements of writing and may undervalue children's attempts to discover the purposes of writing and the excitement of authorship. The 1990 HMI report, *The Teaching and Learning of Language and Literacy*, suggested that good primary practice in writing can be seen where 'the partnership between parents and the school extends to writing' and where parents understand and support the work of the school (HMI, 1990).

Following the publication of the survey by Hall *et al.* (1989) on parental help and the 1990 HMI report, a small-scale home–school writing project was initiated with a group of parent volunteers (Browne and Grindrod, 1991). The aims of this project were to capitalize upon the existing goodwill towards writing that parents have, assess the practicalities of setting up a partnership scheme between school and parents that gave children opportunities to practise writing at home, and to introduce parents to a developmental approach to writing. The parents, from a variety of cultural and socio-economic backgrounds, met in groups with the authors. At the meetings they were given information about the nature of writing and a list of ten home writing activities. The ten writing activities that were suggested were:

- giving the child a notebook and pen and leaving the child to use it as she wishes;
- adult and child working together to produce a child-written and child-illustrated book;
- the child making a catalogue of her toys;
- writing a shopping list;
- rewriting and illustrating a favourite story together;
- the child writing a letter to a parent in response to one received from the parent;
- the child writing a recipe that she could cook later;
- keeping a diary;
- the parent writing a book for the child to read;
- the child keeping a photographic record of an outing or a holiday and providing the captions for the photographs.

In addition, parents were asked to share their own writing with their children and to encourage the children to observe them when they wrote. The only instruction that was given to the parents was to make sure that the writing should be the child's own and to insist that the child 'had a go' at all spellings and sentences.

The comments of the parents involved in the project were illuminating. By the end of the project the parents showed that they had a clear grasp of what writing is for and how it might develop. They talked of purposes and audiences. They discussed layout and redrafting and they appeared to be helping their children in a constructive and positive way. They were more able to appreciate the learning that is taking place and that is displayed when a child tries to write without the emphasis on transcription. In short, they could see the benefits of a developmental approach to writing.

Parents at home can provide real contexts for writing, real audiences for writing and give children a range of writing experiences that complement and extend the writing curriculum of the school. The practice that is afforded by writing at home may have a beneficial effect on children's attitudes to writing and their self-esteem as writers. They are given time and encouragement which even in a busy home is probably more intense than that given by a single teacher to individuals in a class of thirty pupils.

This sort of project could become as much a part of school life as parental involvement in helping with reading at home. Schools could produce a small leaflet giving guidance to parents on how to help with writing at home and list a number of practical ideas for activities that parents could try out. This could be a useful exercise for staff to engage in during staff meetings on writing and might update ideas and practice at school. However, a home–school writing project is very intensive and, rather than implementing a long-term scheme, some schools might prefer to organize a writing week or month once a year. During that period all the writing that is done at home could be displayed in the school along with comments from parents and teachers. The display might coincide with an open evening.

Whether parents are involved for a short or a long time with a home writing scheme they may go on to value their children's spontaneous attempts at writing at home more highly and become more sympathetic to the approach at school rather than dismissing developmental writing as 'that rubbish writing that they do at school'.

Conclusion

Parents and carers play a crucial role in their children's learning. To take advantage of what children learn about writing outside school, teachers need to talk to parents about what their children can do. In order to provide coherent learning experiences for children it is important that parents understand how writing is taught at school. When teachers and parents value the contribution that each party makes to children's learning, children will benefit. They will receive a more coherent educational experience in which home and school both play a part.

Questions about parents and writing

Q. What will parents think about teachers not correcting mistakes?
A. Teachers who use a developmental approach to writing do correct children's mistakes, but they rarely correct all the mistakes in one piece of work. They will need to explain to parents about how and why they correct children's writing. Schools and teachers need to explain their policy on writing and to demonstrate the benefits to parents of teaching developmental writing. If parents understand how and what the child is learning they are generally supportive of the school policy.

Q. What do I say to a parent who insists that her child should 'write properly'?
A. First you need to make it clear to the parent that her child is learning to write properly. Then show her examples of the child's writing and point out all the positive features of the writing such as letters that have been formed correctly or spellings that are nearly correct. Show her the statements of attainment in English in the National Curriculum (DES, 1990) and *Children's Work Assessed* (SEAC, 1990) and demonstrate to her how these correlate with her child's work. Since very often parental concern about writing is related to spelling it might be a good idea to talk specifically about spelling. If appropriate, demonstrate how the child's spelling has progressed and explain that as she gets older and more capable her child's spellings will become even closer to the correct versions. To make spelling development clear to parents it might be useful to explain about how children learn to speak. Parents can usually see that when their child was learning to speak the adults around the child did not correct every word that was said but that gradually their child's spoken language grew more correct and understandable. In a similar way writing and spelling change as the child becomes more experienced at writing and receives sensitive intervention from the teacher.

10

Creating a Writing Policy

Introduction

This chapter presents the reader with a sample of a writing policy written for a first school that uses a developmental approach to writing. The chapter begins by examining some of the processes that staff will engage in before they can write their own policy. The writing policy itself covers writing, spelling and handwriting. It is not meant to be prescriptive but may act as a model for those engaged in producing a writing policy for school.

Before writing the policy

The purpose of a policy is to guide the practice of those who work with pupils in the school, to provide governors and other outside agencies with a statement of teaching aims and intentions, and to satisfy statutory requirements. These audiences may influence the way in which a policy is written. It will need to be clear and concise and may differ from guidelines for teachers which schools may have in addition to their policy.

Embarking on writing a policy presents schools with the opportunity of reviewing current practice and deciding whether or not changes are required. When the decision is made to produce a policy the headteacher and the rest of the staff may meet and discuss current writing practice in the school. The teachers may spend a few weeks reviewing their own practice and observing the children writing. As a result of their observations they may be able to make a list of the good and bad features of their current practice. They may then go on to examine the resources for writing that they use in the classroom and note any omissions. They may also reflect on their own strengths and weaknesses as teachers of writing. These observations and reflections need to be shared with the whole staff group. The staff may then consider what their aims for writing are for the children that they teach. This will necessitate whole staff agreement. By comparing the current writing curriculum with the aims it should be possible to identify any deficiencies in terms of practice, resources and knowledge. It is at this stage that the headteacher may decide to provide opportunities for in-service training and to purchase more resources for writing. Work on producing the writing policy may now begin. The staff may generate a list of headings of the areas that should be included in the policy. In a large school teachers may be asked to take responsibility for certain sections of the policy. In a smaller school the writing of the policy may lie primarily with the headteacher and the English post holder. As the writing proceeds, the contents of the policy should be shared with all the staff. It is essential that everyone agrees and is aware of what is contained within the policy since everyone will be expected to teach in accordance with what has been written. As one of the audiences for all school policies is governors, they will need to be given a copy of the policy as it approaches its final draft. This will give them the opportunity to consider whether they agree with the contents and the opportunity to make suggestions or comments. The policy may then be revised in the light of these contributions. When the policy is complete it should be shared with all members of staff, including welfare assistants, students and anyone that works with the children in the school.

A sample writing policy

Introduction

This policy outlines the way in which writing is taught at Bluebell First School. It is intended that it should be read and adhered to by all those involved in the teaching of writing.

We believe that children learn best when they take an active part in their own learning, when they are aware of the reasons for what they are learning and when they are supported in their learning. For these reasons we use a developmental approach to writing. Spelling and handwriting are best learnt within the context of children's everyday writing. It is not necessary to have separate sessions for these two aspects of writing.

Our aims for the children's writing development are guided by the attainment targets and Programmes of Study laid down for English in the National Curriculum.

Aims

The aims of teaching writing at Bluebell First School are to:

- extend the knowledge and understanding of writing that children bring to school;
- foster a positive attitude towards writing;

- help children understand that writing conveys meaning;
- enable children to understand the reasons for writing;
- develop writing for a variety of audiences and in a variety of styles;
- enhance all children's competence at writing.

The development of writing

When children start school they should be given the opportunity to demonstrate what they know about writing. In the first instance the prime aim is to develop positive attitudes to writing. All children should be encouraged to 'have a go' at writing. Teachers work with whatever the children produce by asking the children to read back what they have written and by giving the children correct models of writing that can be compared with their own version. As the children's writing becomes more readable the teacher may begin to focus on one or two aspects of transcription, for example word spaces or the correct spelling of one or two words. As children grow in competence they should be expected to write more and should write and redraft their work, paying attention to organization, use of language, purpose and audience. The emphasis on transcription should never be at the expense of discussing the choice of words, detail, organization and structure of what has been written. As a general aim children should be expected to progress in writing in accordance with statements of attainment for writing, handwriting and spelling. It would be unwise to attach particular levels to particular ages of children, but teachers need to bear in mind that most seven-year-olds should be producing writing that shows achievement at level two or above.

Organizing for writing

It is easier for the teacher to give support to each child's needs as a writer if only one or two groups are engaged in writing at one time. Occasionally there may be times when all the class is writing at the same time, for example during a special book-making project. Children may also be organized in collaborative mixed-ability groups and pairs for some writing activities. Shared writing with the whole class or with groups of pupils is a useful way of demonstrating all the processes that are used when writing. It can be used to introduce young children to the conventions of print, and older children to ways of planning, drafting, and redrafting. The organization for writing should always complement the nature of the task.

Writing for different purposes and different audiences

Writing at school should always have a purpose that is made clear to the children. It should cover the range of uses for writing that exist, including personal, factual, expressive and imaginative. Children should be encouraged to make notes when carrying out practical tasks and to produce labels and captions for the classroom. Wherever possible, children's writing should have an audience that goes beyond the teacher, such as older and younger children, children in the class, family members, and other outside audiences.

Resources for writing

The classroom should give children the message that writing is a normal activity which they are welcome to take part in. Children should see the same kinds of writing that they see at home, such as lists, greeting cards, notes and letters. Children also need to see new types of writing such as name labels, self-made books, registers and notices. For children to become successful and competent writers and to join in the writing environment, they require a number of essential resources, such as pencils, writing pens, thick and thin felt-pens, crayons, chalks and pastels. In addition, a typewriter or word-processing programme should be available for pupils to use. Pupils should be encouraged to understand that different implements should be used for different sorts of writing, for example thick felt-pens for writing notices, writing pens for final drafts, and pencils for first drafts. Children should be provided with notebooks, class-made books, card, different sorts of paper, and first-draft books for their writing. These resources should be made available in a variety of situations such as a writing corner, the home corner and as part of interactive displays. As children become more proficient writers, dictionaries and thesauruses should be provided. First drafts of writing can be kept in the children's trays but final copies should be placed in the finished work tray, discussed with the teacher, mounted on black paper and then stored in their completed work or writing folders. Erasers should never be used when children are writing.

Spelling

Spelling is only one part of the writing process; it is not the most important part and should not be overemphasized. Children should always be encouraged to have a go at spellings. The teaching of spelling should arise from what children write and be linked to individual children's needs. Correct spelling is taught by the 'look, cover, remember, write, check' method. The reception and Year 1 children may have access to simple dictionaries and word banks, while Year 2 and Year 3 children can begin to use more complicated dictionaries and thesauruses.

Handwriting

Handwriting is only one aspect of writing. The aim should be to teach children to write legibly, fluently and with reasonable speed. To this end children need to be shown correct pencil grip and letter formation. Help with handwriting should arise from how children write. Not every piece of writing children produce needs to be perfect, but teachers should emphasize attention to good presentation when children are writing final drafts. All final drafts should be written with writing pens. Teachers should be alert to the difficulties that left-handed writers may have and make special provision for them. When demonstrating writing to left-handers the teacher should use her left hand. Children in Year 2 and Year 3 who are forming their letters correctly should be introduced to a simple form of cursive script. The teachers should always remember that their writing provides a model for children.

Writing and reading
Good readers are not necessarily good writers; however, as children gain more experience of print through reading it is likely that their writing will improve. In the course of reading, young children can develop their writing since they will be learning about written language. Attending to the details of print in reading will help children with the transcriptional elements of writing such as knowledge about letters, presentation and spelling. Reading will also provide children with ideas about composition.

Bilingual writers
The teacher's expectations about writing development should be the same for bilingual and monolingual pupils. Children who see scripts other than English in the home and in the environment, or who are literate in a language other than English, should not be discouraged from producing writing in scripts that are familiar to them. All the writing that children produce shows evidence of their understanding of the purpose and form of writing. Monolingual pupils should be encouraged to value writing in languages other than English.

Children who find writing difficult
Some children will find writing difficult and may need extra help and support. However, the writing curriculum should be the same for all children but the tasks can be differentiated in terms of outcome or presentation. Sometimes it may be beneficial for less able writers to work with a more competent writer.

Writing and equal opportunities
Teachers should ensure that the writing activities they present to children are appropriate to the needs and interests of girls as well as boys. Teachers' expectations about the presentation of work should be the same for all the children in the class.

Assessment and record-keeping

Most assessment takes place as the teacher works with the children and their writing on a daily basis. More formal evidence of assessment forms part of the literacy record for each child. Teachers should collect samples of children's writing, observations of children as they are writing, records of writing conferences, comments from parents about their child as a writer and comments from any other teachers who see children writing. These should be included in the child's record. Wherever possible, children should be involved in assessing their own writing. Children's assessments may be attached to the samples that the teacher collects. In some cases children may select a best piece of writing to be included in their record. Judgements about children's work should be made with reference to the National Curriculum attainment targets for writing, handwriting, spelling and presentation, the needs of the child and suggestions for the child's future writing development. Year 2 pupils will be assessed using the standard assessments tasks (SATs). The results of these tests should be added to the child's records.

Parents and writing

Parents should be kept informed of their child's writing development, both formally, through parents evenings and reports, and at other times if the parent or the teacher wishes to discuss the child's writing. When children start school, parents should be asked about their child's writing experiences. Suggestions about how parents can help with their child's writing at home are given when their children start school and in the course of curriculum evenings. Parents are also invited into school to help with a range of activities including writing.

Bibliography

Ahlberg, A. (1980) *Mrs Plug the Plumber*, Puffin, Harmondsworth.

Barrs, M., Ellis, S., Hester, H. and Thomas, A. (1990) *Patterns of Learning: The Primary Language Record and the National Curriculum*, CLPE, London.

Barrs, M. and Thomas, A. (eds.) (1991) *The Reading Book*, CLPE, London.

Bissex, G. (1980) *GNYS AT WRK: A Child Learns to Write and Read*, Harvard University Press, Massachusetts.

Bissex, G. (1984) The child as teacher, in H. Goelman, A. Oberg and F. Smith (eds.) *Awakening To Literacy*, The University of Victoria Symposium on Children's Responses to a Literate Environment: Literacy Before Schooling. Heinemann, London.

Browne, A. and Grindrod, R. (1991) Parental involvement in writing, in C. Harrison and E. Ashworth (eds.) *Celebrating Literacy: Defending Literacy*, Basil Blackwell, Oxford.

Burningham, J. (1980) *The Shopping Basket*, Jonathan Cape, London.

Bussis, A., Chittenden, E. and Klausner, E. (1985) *Inquiry into Meaning: An Investigation of Learning to Read*. Erlbaum, Hillsdale, NJ.

Chapman, G. and Robson, P. (1991) *Making Books*, Simon & Schuster, London.

Clay, M. (1975) *What Did I Write?* Heinemann Educational Books, London.

Clover, J. and Gilbert, S. (1984) Parental involvement in the development of language, *Multi-Ethnic Education Review*, Vol. 3, no 1, pp. 6–10.

Cotton, P. (1991) How important are good models of writing in the development of early literacy? Can we learn from our French neighbours? in C. Harrison and E. Ashworth (eds.) *Celebrating Literacy: Defending Literacy*, Basil Blackwell, Oxford.

Cummins, J. (1984) *Bilingualism and Special Education: Issues in Assessment and Pedagogy*. Multilingual Matters, Clevedon.

Czerniewska, P. (1992) *Learning about Writing*, Blackwell, Oxford.

DES (Department of Education and Science) (1988) *Report of the Task Group on Assessment and Testing* (TGAT Report), HMSO, London.

DES (Department of Education and Science) (1989) *English in the National Curriculum*, HMSO, London.

DES (Department of Education and Science) (1990) *English in the National Curriculum (No. 2)*, HMSO, London.

DFE (Department for Education) (1992) *The Education (National Curriculum)*

(Assessment Arrangements For English, Mathematics, Science, Technology, History And Geography) (Key Stage 1) Order 1992, Circular 12/92, HMSO, London.

Dulay, M., Burt, M. and Krashen, S. (1982) *Language Two*, Oxford University Press.

Dyson, A. H. (1983) The role of oral language in early writing processes, *Research in the Teaching of English*, vol. 17, no. 1, pp. 1–29.

Epstein, D. and Sealey, A. (1990) *Where it really matters . . .*, Development Education Centre, Birmingham.

Fernald, G. M. (1943) *Remedial Techniques in Basic School Subjects*, McGraw Hill, New York.

Ferreiro, E. and Teberosky, A. (1979) *Literacy before Schooling*, Heinemann Educational Books, Portsmouth, NH.

Goodman, Y. (1986) Writing Development in Young Children. Gnosis, No. 8., March.

Goodman, Y. (1990) The development of initial literacy, in R. Carter (ed.) *Knowledge about Language and the Curriculum: The LINC Reader*, Hodder & Stoughton, London.

Gorman, T., White, J., Brooks, G. and English, F. (1989) *Language for Learning*, A summary report on the 1988 APU surveys of language performance, HMSO, London.

Graves, D. (1983) *Writing: Teachers and Children at Work*, Heinemann Educational Books, London.

Hall, N. (1987) *The Emergence of Literacy*, Hodder & Stoughton, London.

Hall, N., Hemming, G., Hann, H. and Crawford, L. (1989) *Parental Views on Writing and the Teaching of Writing*, Department of Education Studies, Manchester Polytechnic.

Hester, H. (1983) *Stories in the Multilingual Classroom*, Harcourt Brace Jovanovich Publishers, London.

HM Government (1988) *Education Reform Act*, HMSO, London.

HMI (Her Majesty's Inspectorate) (1990) *The Teaching and Learning of Language and Literacy*, HMSO, London.

ILEA (Inner London Education Authority) (1985) *Improving Primary Schools* (The Thomas Report), ILEA, London.

Jarman, C. (1979) *Developing Handwriting Skills*, Blackwell, Oxford.

Johnson, P. (1990) *A Book of One's Own, Developing Literacy through Making Books*, Hodder & Stoughton, London.

Melser, J. and Cowley, J. (1980) *Mrs Wishy Washy*, Story Chest Large Read – Together Books, E. J. Arnold, Walton-on-Thames.

National Writing Project (1989a) *Becoming a Writer*, Thomas Nelson, Walton-on-Thames.

National Writing Project (1989b) *Responding to and Assessing Writing*, Thomas Nelson, Walton-on-Thames.

NCC (National Curriculum Council) (1989) *English Non Statutory Guidance*, NCC, York.

NCC (National Curriculum Council) (1990) *English Non Statutory Guidance*, NCC, York.

NCC (National Curriculum Council) (1992) *Starting Out with the National Curriculum*, NCC, York.

Palmer, S. (1991) *Spelling: A Teacher's Survival Kit*, Oliver & Boyd, Harlow.

Peters, M. L. (1985) *Spelling Caught or Taught? A New Look*, Routledge, London.

Peters, M. L. and Cripps, C. (1980) *Catchwords: Ideas for Teaching Spelling*, Harcourt Brace Jovanovich, London.

Potter, F. and Sands, H. (1988) Writing and the new technologies in developing children's writing, in D. Wray *et al.* (eds.), *Bright Ideas Teacher Handbook* Scholastic, Leamington Spa.

Read, C. (1986) *Children's Creative Spelling*, Routledge & Kegan Paul, London.

Sassoon, R. (1990) *Handwriting: The Way to Teach it*, Stanely Thornes (Publishers), Cheltenham.

Savva, H. (1990) The rights of bilingual children, in R. Carter (ed.) *Knowledge about Language and the Curriculum: The LINC Reader*, Hodder & Stoughton, London.

Schermbruker, R. and Daly, N. (1992) *Charlie's House*, Walker, London.

SEAC (Schools Examinations and Assessment Council) (1990) *Children's Work Assessed*, HMSO, London.

Smith, F. (1982) *Writing and the Writer*, Heinemann Educational Books, London.

Spender, D. and Spender, E. (eds.) (1980) *Learning to Lose: Sexism and Education*, Women's Press, London.

Swann, J. (1992) *Girls, Boys and Language*, Blackwell, Oxford.

Swann, J. and Graddol, D. (1988) Gender inequalities in classroom talk, *English in Education*, Vol. 22, no 1, pp. 48–65.

Temple, C., Nathan, R., Burris, N. and Temple, F. (1988) *The Beginnings of Writing* (2nd edn), Allyn & Bacon, London.

Tizard, B. and Hughes, M. (1984) *Young Children Learning: Talking and Thinking at Home and at School*, Fontana, London.

White, J. (1990) Questions of choice and change, in National Writing Project: *What Are Writers Made Of? Issues of Gender*, Thomas Nelson, Walton-on-Thames.

Whitehead, M. (1990) *Language and Literacy in the Early Years*, Paul Chapman Publishing, London.

Willig, C. J. (1990) *Children's Concepts and the Primary Curriculum*, Paul Chapman Publishing, London.

Zolotow, C. (1972) *William's Doll*, Harper & Row, New York.

Index

LANGUAGE AND LITERACY IN THE EARLY YEARS 2/E

Marian R. Whitehead

The **Second Edition** has been **revised** and **updated** to reflect the changes since the first edition was published – not only insights into language, literacy and child development, but also new huge changes in the early years environment, typified by The National Curriculum, desirable learning outcomes, baseline assessment, and the just-4s in primary classrooms.

1 85396 341 0 Paperback 208pp 1997

THE NURSERY TEACHER IN ACTION

Teaching 3-, 4- and 5-year-olds 2/E

Margaret Edgington
(formerly Margaret Lally)

In this **Second Edition**, the work of the nursery teacher is explored in depth as the author draws on her own experiences as nursery teacher, advisory teacher, nursery school headteacher and specialist consultant, and on the views of teachers working in the field.

1 85396 368 2 Paperback 256pp 1998

STARTING SCHOOL AT FOUR

A Joint Endeavour

Marion Dowling

This book highlights issues concerning the child's first year in school and considers the needs of 4-year-olds. The author sets out the basics of good educational practice for the under-fives.

1 85396 270 8 Paperback 184pp 1995

EDUCATION 3-5 2/E

Marion Dowling

The **Second Edition** of this widely-used book blends a practical approach to nursery work with a consideration of research which highlights the best practice. Relevant to all in pre-school and early primary education.

1 85396 166 3 Paperback 240pp 1992

PLANNING FOR EARLY LEARNING 2/E
Educating Young Children
Victoria Hurst

In this **Second Edition**, the author sets out how practitioners can structure and organise their thinking about early education and curriculum, so that they can support and extend children's learning and development. She also shows how practitioners can judge the effectiveness of their educational provision and learn more about the education of young children.

1 85396 344 5 Paperback 176pp 1997

ASSESSMENT IN EARLY CHILDHOOD EDUCATION
edited by Geva M. Blenkin and A. V. Kelly

This book identifies the essential features of forms of assessment which will be genuinely supportive of education in the early years; helps teachers in their research for such forms; and evaluates the likely impact of the systems of external assessment currently being imposed.

1 85396 153 1 Paperback 200pp 1992

THE NATIONAL CURRICULUM AND EARLY LEARNING
An Evaluation
edited by Geva M. Blenkin and A. V. Kelly

The authors evaluate the impact of the 1988 Education Act which instituted The National Curriculum in England and Wales, especially in the light of the conflicting claims which are emerging.

1 85396 241 4 Paperback 256pp 1994

THREADS OF THINKING
Young Children Learning and the Role of Early Education
Cathy Nutbrown

The author presents evidence of continuity and progression in young children's thinking and shows, with detailed observations, that young children are able and active learners. She considers aspects of children's patterns of learning and thinking (or schemas) and demonstrates clearly how children learn in an active, dynamic and creative way.

1 85396 217 1 Paperback 176pp 1994

RECURRING THEMES IN EDUCATION
Tina Bruce, Anne Findlay, Jane Read and Mary Scarborough

This book explores six recurring educational themes, which each generation of educators needs to address. This book provides a forward-looking and up-to-date perspective in relation to Froebel's principles.

1 85396 264 3 Paperback 160pp 1995

**Complete catalogue of Early Years titles
available on request.**